1988

The Athlete's Guide.

Increasing Strength, Power and Agility

The Athlete's Guide:

Increasing Strength, Power and Agility

James A. Baley

PARKER PUBLISHING COMPANY, INC.
West Nyack, N.Y.

This book is dedicated to my Mother
who was a champion in many ways

Originally published as

Illustrated Guide to Developing Athletic Strength, Power and Agility

Reward Edition . . . . September 1982

Library of Congress Cataloging in Publication Data

Baley, James A
   Illustrated guide to developing athletic
strength, power and agility.

   1. Physical education and training. 2. Exercise.
I. Title. II. Title: Developing athletic
strength, power, and agility.
GV711.5.B34   796.4'07   76-23440

WHAT THIS BOOK CAN DO FOR YOU

Have you wished that you could throw with greater speed, jump higher, run faster, hit harder, throw further, have greater endurance, be able to lift heavier weights or bend further? How many athletes have envied the stronger, more enduring or more flexible athlete who has beaten them? Many have secretly assumed that their victor has been endowed with superior athletic ability. They did not realize that practice on the skills of a sport is, in most cases, only half of the program leading toward championship performance. They did not realize that the apparent physical endowment necessary for championship level performance might well be the result of the proper physical conditioning program. Through a good physical conditioning program, they can change their physical equipment so that they can jump higher, run and throw faster and further. This book shows these would-be champions and top flight performers how to change their physical equipment so that their performance will greatly improve. Basketball players will be able to jump inches higher to recover more rebounds, and they'll be as aggressive at the end of the game as they were at its beginning. Football linemen will hit with greater explosive force. Backfield men will be able to avoid would-be tacklers because they'll be able to stop, start and change directions more quickly. Baseball players will be able to jump higher to catch more line drives, bat with greater power and throw faster and further to put out more runners. The forehand and backhand drives and serves of tennis, squash and paddleball players will whistle over the nets with greater speed giving opponents little time to return the ball. Gymnasts will find themselves with sufficient strength to do press-ups, levers and the crucifix. They'll be able to do splits and backbends and assume piked positions tight enough to do double somersaults. Volleyball players will be able to spike with tremendous force. Wrestlers will effect escapes more easily, will be able to break many of their opponents' holds and will muscle their opponent to a pin.

This book tells you, in simple, easy to follow language, how to develop the specific physical qualities needed to perform at championship levels. A total of 31 weight training exercises, 46 strength and power building exercises with an inexpensive isometric belt, 36 isometric exercises in which a beach towel is used, 42 isometric exercises which may be done anywhere at any time, 39 exercises to improve dynamic and static balance, 49 exercises to improve range of motion, programs to develop agility and programs to develop endurance such as interval training, grass drills, aerobics, progressive rhythmic non-stop exercises, cycling, rope skipping, circuit training and wind sprints are all described and illustrated through over 270 pictures and diagrams. Fourteen distinct sports exercise programs are presented that develop the muscle groups and specific motor fitness qualities demanded in these sports.

Jim Baley

CONTENTS

**3   Isometric Exercises with a Beach Towel, Partner and
Without Equipment • 67**

Isometric Exercises with a Towel • Exercises for the Arms and Shoulder
Girdle

*1. Military Press • 2. Press Behind Neck • 3. Supine Press • 4. Arm
Depressor • 5. Front Curl • 6. Reverse Curl • 7. Standing Pull-Up •
8. Forward Extended Arm Depressor • 9. Sideward Extended Arm
Depressor • 10. Forward Extended Arm Elevator • 11. Sideward
Extended Arm Elevator • 12. Pole Vaulter's Exercise •
13. Swimmer's Exercise*

Exercises for the Legs and Feet

*14. Sitting Leg Extensor • 15. Sitting Plantar Flexor • 16. Prone
, Leg Extensor • 17. Supine Hip Flexor • 18. Sitting Leg Abductor •
19. Sitting Foot Abductor • 20. Side Leg Flexor • 21. Side Leg
Extensor • 22. Sitting Leg Adductor • 23. Sitting Foot Adductor •
24. Sitting Dorsi Flexor*

Exercises for the Trunk and Neck

*25. Chest Pull • 26. Head Forward Push • 27. Head Backward
Push • 28. Head Sideward Push • 29. Head Turn • 30. Supine Extended Arm Elevator • 31. Pull Over • 32. Bent Over Rowing Exercise • 33. Dead Lift • 34. Suitcase Life*

Exercises for the Wrists and Hands

35. Wrist Front Curl • 36. Wrist Reverse Curl

Isometric Exercises Without Equipment • Exercises for the Arms and
Shoulders Girdle

*37. Extended Arm Elevator • 38. Extended Arm Depressor •
39. Flexed Arm Elevator • 40. Flexed Arm Depressor •
41. Forward Extended Arm Sideward Mover • 42. Arm Extensor •
43. Front Curl on a Desk • 44. Reverse Curl on Desk • 45. Arm
Depressor on Desk • 46. Arm Depressor on Chair • 47. Chair Lift •
48. Parade Rest Pull • 49. Overhead Pull • 50. Sideward Arm
Elevator • 51. Sideward Arm Depressor • 52. Forward Extended
Arm Elevator • 53. Pull Over • 54. Resisted Push-Up*

Exercises for the Legs and Feet

*55. Sitting Knee Adductor • 56. Sitting Leg Adductor • 57. Sitting
Leg Adductor • 58. Dorsi-Flexor on Desk • 59. Foot Abductor •
60. Foot Adductor • 61. Rise on Toes in Door Frame • 62. Sitting
Knee Extensor with Partner • 63. Sitting Knee Flexor with Partner •
64. Ankle Eversion and Inversion with Partner*

7   Individualized Exercise Programs for Different Sports (cont.)

for Tennis, Badminton, Squash, Paddleball and Handball

Conditioning Exercises for Gymnasts

Strength Exercises for Gymnasts • Endurance Exercises for Gymnasts • Agility for Gymnasts • Balance for Gymnasts • Flexibility for Gymnasts

Conditioning for Volleyball

Strength for Volleyball Players • Endurance Exercises for Volleyball Players • Agility for Volleyball Players • Flexibility for Volleyball Players

Conditioning for Sprinters

Strength and Power for Sprinters • Endurance for Sprinters • Flexibility for Sprinters

Conditioning for the Throwing Events in Track and Field

Strength and Power for Throwing Events in Track and Field • Flexibility Exercises for Throwing Events in Track and Field

Conditioning Exercises for Pole Vaulters

Strength and Power Exercises for the Pole Vaulter • Flexibility Exercises for Pole Vaulters

Conditioning Exercises for Lacrosse Players

Strength and Power Exercises for Lacrosse Players • Endurance Exercises for Lacrosse Players • Flexibility Exercises for Lacrosse

Conditioning Exercises for Soccer Players

Strength Exercises for Soccer Players • Endurance Exercises for Soccer Players • Flexibility Exercises for Soccer Players

Wrestling

Strength Exercises for Wrestlers • Endurance Exercises for Wrestlers • Flexibility Exercises for Soccer • Circuit Training • Grass Drills • Rope Skipping • Jogging • Balance Exercises for Wrestlers • Flexibility Exercises for Wrestlers

1

PROCEDURES FOR DEVELOPING ATHLETIC STRENGTH AND POWER

PRINCIPLES FOR DEVELOPING STRENGTH AND POWER

Various physical and emotional characteristics are essential for championship level performance in different sports. The great basketball player is frequently very tall, agile, with good speed, has outstanding hand-eye coordination and the ability to keep cool under emotional pressure. The great football lineman most often has inherited a large, heavy bony framework which can accomodate a substantial amount of muscle and is aggressive and enjoys body contact. Champion gymnasts are usually average or below average in height with relatively light bones. They enjoy indirect (non-contact) forms of competition and competition with their own previous performances. National and world champion swimmers usually have long levers (arms and legs), big paddles (hands and feet), are light boned (greater buoyancy), enjoy physical fatigue and derive a feeling of achievement in persisting in spite of the fatigue.

SOMATOTYPE

Although champions in football, basketball, gymnastics, and swimming (and in other sports) often have important basic genetic differences in height, density and thickness of bones, size of body parts relative to other parts (the hands and feet of the swimmer for example) and in psychological characteristics, they have one thing in common. They all have great strength and power. They develop great strength because they are all high in the inherited quality called mesomorphy. Mesomorphs are characterized by broad shoulders, relatively narrow hips, squareness of head and ample muscular development.

There are two other body types—ectomorph and endomorph. Ectomorphs are characterized by a large amount of skin of surface area relative to their total body volume. These thin linear types feel cold before their thicker friends. They have more surface area relative to total body volume from which to lose heat. Their body is like a radiator from which heat can be quickly conducted. Anyone who has watched little children swimming early in the summer has noticed that the thick fat ones are the last to leave the cold water and the thin ones are the first to show "goose bumps," blue lips and shivering. The endomorph is characterized by relatively large abdominal volume, roundness, softness and fat. Endomorphs have an intestinal tract which is two feet longer than average. This enables them to get more nutrition from the food they ingest. This longer cavity also requires more food to fill. Generally, people high in endomorphy are not successful in athletics, do not enjoy physical activity and do not adapt to physical stress very well.

Everyone possesses some degree of each of the three components of body type—endomorphy, mesomorphy and ectomorphy. Shot putters, hammer throwers, football linemen, channel swimmers and weight lifters are above average in endomorphy and low in ectomorphy. Distance runners, long jumpers, high jumpers, and basketball players are above average in ectomorphy and below average in endomorphy. But all of these, and all other athletes, are above average in mesomorphy because in almost all sports strength is the most important single quality for success. Champion athletes are almost always considerably above average in strength. A high degree of mesomorphy is essential to the development of a large amount of strength. Consequently, the coach of any high school athletic team, the coach of children below high school age or the coach of small college teams who is unable to recruit players of proven ability, should look first for boys high in mesomorphy. Then, because strength, power, and muscular endurance are most easy to develop and they are most important to high level performance in all sports, he should develop their strength, power, and muscular endurance.

Dr. James Counsilman, coach of swimming at Indiana University, has coached scores of national and Olympic swimming champions, and he recognized the importance of strength and muscular endurance early in his coaching career. When coaching swimming at State University of New York in Cortland, he was unable to recruit the better high school swimming champions. He found a young man in his Beginning Swimming class who couldn't swim but possessed great muscular endurance as a result of having done crew. This young man went on to win the world championship in the mile and the 440. This true story points out the importance and priority of physical fitness in the development of championship level athletic ability. The first consideration in the selection of team members is: Does the boy or young man possess the specific inherited or genetic characteristics required for success in the particular sport, such as body proportions, body type (somatotype), psychologic characteristics, hand-eye coordination, length of body levers. The coach must try to select boys high in mesomorphy because it is of prime importance to success in athletics and it is a prerequisite to the development of strength. Next, optimal strength must be developed. This chapter presents the latest scientific principles, plus a large number of exercises designed to develop the strength, power and muscular endurance necessary for championship athletic performance.

DIFFERENCES BETWEEN TRAINING AND PRACTICE SESSIONS

The objectives of practice sessions are to improve the specific skills involved in a sport, to improve teamwork and team strategies and to increase understanding of the sport. There is a great deal of time spent in listening to explanations and instructions, watching demonstrations, walking through drills, and setting up formations. Practice aims to improve control of muscular activity by the nervous system. Although some fatigue is experienced by the participants, little improvement in the specific qualities of physical fitness (strength, power, endurance, agility, flexibility and balance) results for competitive athletes in comparison to the amount which can be developed through a training or conditioning program specifically designed to improve the qualities of athletic physical fitness. Athletic skills must be built upon a strong foundation of physical fitness. The greater the general qualities of strength, power, endurance, flexibility, and agility, the more quickly will the specific skills be learned and once learned the better will be the performance. In training or conditioning, a specific kind of stress is applied to the body to elicit a specific kind of adaptation. To increase endurance many repetitions of a movement against little resistance are done to produce cardiac and respiratory stress. Examples are jogging, cycling, swimming for distance or calisthenics. To increase strength and power few repetitions against great resistance which the muscles can barely overcome are done. Examples are weight training and isometric exercises. To increase range of motion or flexibility, the tendons and other connective tissues are stressed through stretching to the point of pain. Specific exercises must be done to develop the specific qualities (strength, power, endurance, flexibility, agility, and balance) in the specific proportions, and for the specific activity. Strength and power must be developed where needed.

STRESS

All living things either adapt to stresses to which they are subjected or they die. If the stresses are excessive and too suddenly imposed, illness or death results, but if the imposed stress is within tolerance and if the amount of stress is gradually increased, adaptations are made which make possible handling of the stress. This is what conditioning or training is. The weight trainer begins by lifting a weight with which he can barely eke out 5-6 repetitions. He must make a great effort to lift the weight the last time. After several exercise sessions his muscles adapt by becoming stronger permitting him to do 8-10 repetitions. At this time, he increases the resistance (weight) against his muscles by an amount permitting only 5-6 repetitions and builds up over several exercise sessions to 8-10 repetitions. In jogging, he increases the distance jogged or the speed at which a measured, distance is covered—or both—at each exercise session as the heart muscle, blood vessels and respiratory systems make adaptations to the imposed stress by becoming more efficient in performance of their functions. To increase flexibility, the athlete stretches his joints to the point of pain at each exercise session and the tendons and other connective tissues adapt by becoming more elastic.

We see this phenomenon of adaptation to stress not only in athletic training or conditioning but in many other areas as well. Man has adapted to life at sea level and at mile high altitudes with its rarified atmosphere. He lives at an altitude of 9000 feet above sea level in Mexico City and at or below sea level in Salt Lake City or next to the Dead Sea. Many coaches and sports writers anticipated that times in the endurance events in the Olympic Games held in Mexico City would not equal those made in previous Olympic Games. They overlooked the marvelous adaptive powers of the human body. Athletes conditioned at high altitudes for many weeks previous to the Olympic Games not only equaled but surpassed previous performances.

Stress within adaptive amounts should be sought out—not avoided—by those people who wish to become stronger, tougher, and more enduring.

Function makes an organ. Muscles which are not used atrophy. When the heart muscle is not stressed, it too atrophies. Gymnasts develop callouses on their hands and dancers develop callouses on their feet as an adaptation to the friction imposed. Even bone tissue will atrophy when not used and hypertrophy as a result of increased use. For example, if a child is stricken by poliomyelitis and the innervation to one leg is lost, the affected leg will not grow apace with the unaffected leg and the bones of the affected leg will be shorter and thinner even though the polio virus has no direct effect upon bone, circulation, or muscular tissue.

THE MUSCULAR SYSTEM AND
EFFECTS OF MUSCULAR ACTIVITY

There are 656 skeletal muscles in the body. Each of these has a specialized function to perform. Together, they make up forty-two percent of the total weight in the male and thirty-six percent in the female.

The basic unit of the muscular system is the muscle fiber. Muscle fibers are grouped together to form a *motor unit*. A motor unit may consist of as few as three muscle fibers (extrinsic muscles of the eyes) or as many as a hundred or more (muscles of the thighs). Each motor unit contracts as a unit since all its fibers are innervated simultaneously by one motor nerve. Where precise and delicate movements are needed such as in the fingers, tongue, lips or eyes, motor units consist of only a few muscle fibers but where gross movements are called for as in the thighs, back or abdomen, motor units consist of many muscle fibers. Each motor unit has its own minimal threshold of excitability. The muscle fibers in some motor units will contract with a small stimulus while those in other motor units require stronger stimuli and those in some motor units will not contract unless a very strong stimuli is presented. As the nervous stimulus increases in intensity, a greater number of motor units become activated. All the muscle fibers in each motor unit contract according to the "all or none" law, that is, if they contract at all, they contract maximally. When picking up a peanut only the muscle fibers in motor units with a small minimal threshold of excitability will contract. When making a maximal contraction, as in lifting a weight which can be barely lifted or as in making a maximal isometric contraction, the muscle fibers in all the motor units will contract. The ability of skeletal muscles to adjust the intensity of their contraction to the resistance offered is known as the *grading* mechanism of muscle. The number of muscle fibers and motor units remains constant throughout life. Increases in strength occur because the individual muscle fibers become stronger. Muscle fibers not used atrophy. This is evidenced when wearing a cast on the leg. Although the cast fits snuggly when it is first put on, after a time, the hand can be inserted between the cast and the leg. The cast didn't stretch. The muscles of the legs shrank—atrophied.

If a peanut were lifted a billion times each day there would be no increases in strength because muscle fibers in the motor units with a high minimal threshold of excitability would not be used and they would atrophy. There would, however, be an increase in the capillarization and vascularization of the exercised area which would contribute to increased muscular endurance. When muscle fibers contract many times at a rate beyond the efficiency of the circulatory system, fatigue products accumulate at the nerve synapses and within the muscle cells. This elevates the threshold of excitability of the motor unit to a point higher than the threshold of excitability of some other motor units. The muscle fibers in the first motor unit then cease to contract and secure a needed rest period while the muscle fibers in other motor units with just slightly higher thresholds of excitability take over the work until those in the first motor unit recover.

The preceding explanation of the physiology of muscular contraction explains why use of heavy resistances which mandates few repetitions must be done to increase strength and power. It also explains why as the resistance is decreased and the number of repetitions is increased, increases in strength become smaller while increases in muscular endurance become greater. This means that exercise sessions can be planned to develop the amount of strength, power and muscular endurance needed in the sport for which the participant is conditioning or training. We now have enough understanding of the physiology of exercise to prescribe pretty much as the physician prescribes drugs for the treatment of illness. For example, in power events such as the shot put, hammer throw, discus, javelin, high jump, long jump, sprint swimming and running events fewer repetitions against greater resistance for the muscles principally involved in the sports action should be done consistant with the need to hold body weight down in some sports such as in gymnastics and high jumping. Jumpers and sprint runners need their power principally in the legs, sprint swimmers need strong arms and legs; gymnasts need strong arms.

Middle distance runners or swimmers do not apply as much force against the ground or water as do sprinters but do more repetitions of the movement, requiring less power but more muscular endurance. They, therefore, must do more repetitions against less resistance. In doing so, they will improve the blood supply to the exercised muscle. It has been found that exercised animals have forty to forty-five percent more capillaries in muscle tissue than do sedentary animals. This increase in the capillary bed makes possible movement of a greater volume of blood per minute through the area. This in turn, makes possible a more rapid removal of fatigue products and carbon dioxide from the muscle cells and transport of a greater supply per minute of oxygen and nutrients to the muscle cells so that the onset of physiologic fatigue does not occur as rapidly.

Some people can develop considerably more strength than others. The reason for this is not fully understood at the present time. However, some of the reasons are the following:

1. Those with heavier bones can accomodate more muscle.
2. There may be differences in the strength of will and in degree of motivation.
3. The muscles of some people may insert on the bone further from the joint than in others. This would provide a better mechanical advantage for the contracting muscle.

All levers in the human body are third class levers with the weight or resistance on one end and the fulcrum on the other. The application of force is between these two points. The distance from the fulcrum to the application of force (force arm) times the force equals the distance from the fulcrum to the application of weight or resistance (resistance arm) times the weight. In a third class lever, the resistance arm is always longer than the force arm and third class levers require that the force always exceed the resistance or weight to be lifted. This is especially true in the human body because the force arm is always very short relative to the resistance arm. In addition, the line of pull of the muscle is at a right angle to the long axis of the bone it is moving for only a brief moment during the contraction of the muscle. During the first part of a muscle's contraction its line of pull is almost parallel to the long axis of the bone. Although this provides a stabilizing force to prevent dislocation; it also makes it necessary that the muscle generate tremendous force in order to initiate flexion of the joint. Human levers favor speed at the cost of force. They enable the body part to be moved very rapidly but also require the generation of a tremendous amount of force. It has been found that three hundred pounds of force must be developed by the deltoid muscle to lift a ten pound weight held in the hand with the arm extended.

From the preceding mechanical and anatomic analysis it can be easily seen why great strength is required to throw a ball, discus or javelin with speed or for some distance, to kick a football or soccer ball, to run or jump or to swing a bat, racquet or lacrosse or hockey stick. All other factors being equal (skill, length of levers, body weight, muscle viscosity, etc.) the greater the athlete's strength, the farther and faster a ball may be thrown; the faster the bat or racquet may be swung; the higher and farther he will jump or vault, and the faster he will propel himself over land or in the water. An athlete can not increase the length of his anatomic levers or change the angle or point of insertion of his tendons but he can increase the force which he can generate by increasing his strength.

TYPES OF MUSCULAR CONTRACTION

Imagine a wrist wrestling match. Jones is pinning Smith. Jones' muscles are undergoing a concentric contraction because they are shortening, that is, the angle at the joint being moved (elbow) becomes smaller and the bone (radius and ulna) being moved approach the one on which they are moving (humerus). This is called a concentric (toward center) contraction. Smith's muscles are undergoing an eccentric (away from center) contraction because they are giving to the force imposed against them. The angle at the joint (elbow) is increasing and the bones of the forearm (radius and ulna) are moving away from the bone on which they are moving (humerus). If neither Jones nor Smith is winning the contest, their muscles are undergoing an isometric or static contraction. The muscles don't know what kind of contraction they are undergoing. Only the brain knows this. The muscles adapt to this stress by becoming stronger. The amount of adaptation (hyper-trophy) is the same whether the contraction is isometric (or static), concentric or eccentric.

SUGGESTIONS AND PRINCIPLES FOR WEIGHT TRAINING AND ISOMETRIC EXERCISE PROGRAMS

Research has presented us with the following suggestions and principles for weight training and isometric exercise programs:

1. It is well to practice exercises, which exert a sharp pull on the muscles and tendons in order to diminish the attenuating influence of the Golgi sensory organs of inhibition. However, these kinds of exercises should be done progressively, that is, the weight (as in the clean and jerk or snatch) should be increased gradually. The job of the Golgi sensory organs is to discharge inhibitory impulses whenever muscle tension rises above their threshold level of stimulus. This serves to stop further increases in muscle tension. Obviously, if these inhibitory impulses can be decreased through conditioning, the muscles will be able to generate greater tension more quickly.

2. Training need not "taper-off." Research has shown no harmful effects as a result of sudden cessation of training efforts.

3. Four training sessions per week appear to be the optimal amount. This should be two heavy resistance days and two light resistance days per week. However, four training sessions per week are not twice as productive as two sessions. Beginners should workout three times per week until their physical condition improves sufficiently to tolerate four sessions per week.

4. Exercise periods of two to three minutes should alternate with rest periods of equal length.

5. Once the desired strength level has been reached, these gains can be retained by exercising once each week.

6. In swimming and in similar events in which the resistance against the muscular effort is small, strength declines during the competitive season. This results in a lack of reserve strength which can limit performance. Athletes in sports of this type need to do strength exercises during the competitive season.

7. During hot weather all possible efforts should be made to guard

against the possibility of heat exhaustion or heat stroke. Heat stroke is a serious condition which can result in death. During exercise sessions light clothing should be worn. Air circulation should be sought. Consumption of water and salt tablets should be encouraged not only previous to and after the exercise sessions but during the exercises session as well. Athletes should be progressively acclimatized to exercising in the heat. Feelings of dizziness, nausea and faintness should not be ignored! They may be symptoms of impending heat stroke or heat exhaustion.

8. Training does not improve coordination. Coordination in a specific skill is improved by practice in that skill.

9. Deep breathing exercises are a waste of time and effort. Inhaled oxygen is simply exhaled if the need for oxygen has not been created in the muscle cells.

10. During maximal muscular effort, the glotis should be kept open (exhale by making an *f-f-f-f* or *s-s-s-s* sound) in order to maintain uniform intrathoracic pressure. During a hard muscular contraction the thoracic and abdominal muscles contract to stabilize the bony framework. When the breath is held, the intrathoracic pressure is increased which produces pressure on the venae cava slowing down the return of blood to the heart with the result that the heart has little or no blood to pump. The systolic pressure first rapidly rises to 180 or 220 mm Hg and then just as rapidly falls to 60 mm Hg. The lower pressure could cause a "blackout" or fainting. The high blood pressure could cause rupture of a weak artery. This hasn't happened to an athlete but elderly people straining at the stool (a hard isometric contraction) have suffered cerebrovascular accidents (CVA) or strokes.

11. Strength does not impair coordination or flexibility. Strength is dependent upon the size of muscle fibers. Flexibility is dependent upon the elasticity of noncontractile connective tissue. Coordination is dependent upon the quality of the nervous system and the amount of practice in the specific skill. All of these are separate entities.

12. Mental-emotional states are important to the effectiveness of training sessions. Positive mental/emotional states permit greater effort and consequent greater rewards in terms of improved physical fitness. Work is easier with music. A strong desire to improve makes training easier. Knowledge by the participant that he will not injure or harm himself with great effort will permit him to make maximal efforts.

PROGRESSIVE RESISTANCE EXERCISES

General Procedures

Research indicates that 1-3 repetitions done 3-4 times (sets) with a load which can be done 1-3 times is best for development of strength and that 10-12 repetitions for 3-4 sets with 80% maximum load is best for development of muscular endurance. It is recommended that beginners train three times per week. As fitness and strength improves, the athletes may train four days per week—exercising the upper body one day, the lower body the following day, a day of rest, exercising the upper body the next day, the lower body the following day and then resting for two days. Power cleans a variety of pressing movements and squats should be included in every program.

A rest period of one to two minutes should be taken following each set. Each exercise should be completed in the recommended sequence and in the recommended number of sets before proceeding to the next exercise.

EXERCISES FOR THE ARMS AND SHOULDER GIRDLE

1. Military Press

Grasp the bar in a front grip shoulder width apart and clean it to the shoulders. The feet should be parallel and 12-14 inches apart, knees locked, head up and elbows at the sides. Inhale deeply and with back straight push the bar directly overhead. During the press the muscles of the hips, thighs and abdomen should be contracted (*Figures 1-1 and 1-2*).

Figure 1-2

Figure 1-1

2. Press Behind Neck

This exercise is done in the same manner as the military press except that the grip is slightly wider than shoulder width and the bar is pressed from the base of the neck behind the head (*Figures 1-3 and 1-4*).

Figure 1-3   **Figure 1-4**

3. Seated Military Press

This exercise is done in the same manner as the military press except that the athlete is seated on a bench or box during the press (*Figure 1-5*).

4. Bench Press

The athlete begins lying supine on a bench with his head on the bench. The barbell should be handed to him by two team-mates who lift the barbell, one at each end, and remain in position ready to catch the barbell in the event the athlete loses its balance. The athlete grasps the bar with a front grip slightly wider than shoulder width. His arms are extended. He inhales, lowers the bar to his chest and immediately presses it upward (*Figure 1-6*).

Figure 1-5   **Figure 1-6**

5. Bent Over Rowing

The athlete stands with his feet 12-14 inches apart, his trunk parallel to the floor and grasping the bar at arms length with a front grip slightly wider than shoulder width. He pulls the bar up to his chest and lowers it while keeping his knees locked and his trunk parallel to the floor (*Figure 1-7*).

Figure 1-7

6. Upright Rowing

The athlete. begins in a standing position holding the bar at arms length (arms hanging downward) with a front grip hands 3-6 inches apart. Leading with his elbows, he pulls the bar upward along his body to his chin (*Figures 1-8 and 1-9*).

Figure 1-8　　　　　　　　　　　**Figure 1-9**

7. Front Curl

The athlete starts in a standing position holding the bar with a front grip at arms length directly in front of his hips. Holding his elbows at his sides, he flexes them to bring the bar to his chest and then lowers it to the starting position (*Figures 1-10 and 1-11*).

Figure 1-10　　　　　　　　　　**Figure 1-11**

8. Reverse Curl

This exercise is done in the same manner as the front curl except that a reverse (palms down) grip is used (*Figure 1-12*).

Figure 1-12

9. Lat (Latissmus) Exercise

The athlete begins in a kneeling position or sitting on a bench in front of the lat machine. He grasps the bar at arms' length directly above his head with a front grip and pulls it down until it touches the base of his neck. He should maintain contact with the bench throughout the exercise.

10. Triceps Exercise

The athlete begins in a standing position directly in front of the lat machine with his back toward it. He grasps the bar at chest level with a front grip with his hands 3-6 inches apart. Keeping his elbows in, he pushes the bar downward until his arms are fully extended.

11. Supine Triceps Extension

The athlete begins in a supine position on a bench. He grasps the barbell with a front grip slightly narrower than shoulder width, with the elbows adducted and with the bar resting on the bench above his head; he pulls the bar upward above his head until his elbows are fully extended and then returns to the starting position.

12. Bent Arm Pull Over

The athlete begins from a supine position on a bench with the head beyond the end of the bench. She grasps the bar (which is on the floor) with a front grip behind her head. She then pulls the bar up over her chest and returns it to the floor (*Figures 1-13 and 1-14*).

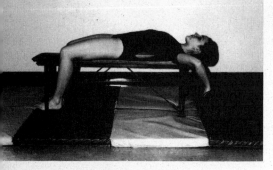
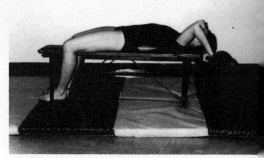

Figure 1-13   **Figure 1-14**

EXERCISES FOR THE WRISTS AND HANDS

13. Front Wrist Curl

The athlete sits on a bench, box or chair with her forearms along her thighs, her hands just beyond her knees and holding the barbell with a front grip. She flexes her wrists and then hyperextends them (*Figures 1-15 and 1-16*).

Figure 1-15   **Figure 1-16**

14. Reverse Wrist Curl

This exercise is done in the same manner as the front wrist curl except that a reverse (palms down) grip is used (*Figure 1-17*).

Figure 1-17

EXERCISES FOR THE LEGS AND FEET

15. Dead Lift

The athlete starts in a squatting position with his thighs parallel to the floor, feet 12-18 inches apart, head up, back angled upward 25-30 degrees and arched, arms extended and hands gripping the bar with a front grip at shoulder width. He inhales and extends his knees and hips to pull the barbell directly upward until it is in front of his hips.

Figure 1-18   Figure 1-19   Figure 1-20

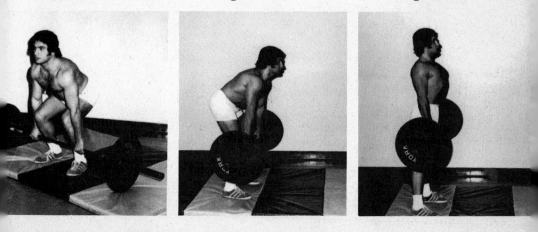

Throughout the lift he keeps his arms extended and avoids rounding his back, flexing his hips and "jerking" the weight off the floor. He then lowers the bar to the floor slowly (*Figures 1-18, 1-19, 1-20*).

16. Power Clean

The starting position and the initial movements are the same as in the dead lift. When the bar reaches a level 4-5 inches above the knees, the athlete rises on his toes and drives his hips upward and forward to accelerate the upward movement of the barbell. At the same time he pulls his elbows up and outward. When the bar is approximately chest high, he bends his knees to drop under the bar and whips his elbows forward and under the bar to catch the bar across his chest and shoulders. He then comes to the erect position to complete the lift. When doing the power clean in series, he flexes his wrists, brings his elbows up and outward and flexes his knees and hips as he brings the barbell back to the floor and his body to the starting position (*Figures 1-21, 1-22, 1-23*).

Figure 1-21   Figure 1-22   Figure 1-23

17. Dead Hang Power Clean

This exercise is done in the same manner as the power clean except that the barbell is not lowered all the way to the floor but only several inches from the floor when it is again cleaned to the chest.

18. Squat

The athlete starts in a standing position with the bar behind his head and across his shoulders. His head is up. His upper back is flat while his lower back is arched. His feet are 12-14 inches apart. He inhales and flexes his knees until his thighs are parallel to the floor and then returns to the erect position. Throughout the exercise, he avoids rounding the back and bouncing out of the squat. If he has difficulty maintaining balance due to lack of flexibility in the tendon of achilles, he is advised to place a block of wood under his heels. He avoids squatting beyond a point where his thighs are below the horizontal because of potential damage to the knee joints (*Figure 1-24*).

19. Front Squat

This exercise is done in the same manner as the squat except that the barbell is held on the chest. To facilitate holding the bar on the chest, the elbows should be held high (*Figure 1-25*).

Figure 1-24

Figure 1-25

20. Back Squat

This exercise is done in the same manner as the squat except that the bar is held behind the legs (*Figure 1-26*).

Figure 1-26

21. Rise on Toes

The athlete begins in a standing position with the barbell either behind his head and across his shoulders or held in front of his hips with his arms extended. He rises up on his toes and lowers back down to his heels. He may come up on the inside of his feet and down on the outside of his feet or visa versa (*Figure 1-27*).

Figure 1-27

22. Leg Curl

Iron boats or a leg extension machine are necessary to execution of this exercise. The athlete begins in a prone position with his legs extended and flexes his knees until his lower legs are vertical and then returns to the starting position.

23. Knee Extensor

Iron boats or a leg extension machine are necessary for the execution of this exercise. The athlete begins from a position sitting on a table with the backs of his knees just over the edge. His lower legs hang downward. He extends his knees until his legs are straight and then lowers them to the starting position.

EXERCISES FOR THE TRUNK AND NECK

24. Shoulder Shrug

The athlete begins in a standing position holding the bar at shoulder width with a front grip in front of his hips with his arms extended. Keeping his arms extended, he shrugs his shoulders upward and backward and returns to the starting position (*Figures 1-28 and 1-29*).

Figure 1-28   Figure 1-29

25. Lateral Rise with Dumbbells

The athlete begins in a standing position holding the dumbbells at his sides with a regular grip with his arms extended. He lifts the dumbbells sideward and above his head and returns to the starting position holding his arms extended throughout the exercise (*Figure 1-30*).

Figure 1-30

26. Forward Raise with Dumbbells

The athlete begins in a standing position holding the dumbbells in a front grip with one arm extended overhead and the other extended downward. He elevates one dumbbell overhead as he lowers the other holding his arms extended throughout the exercise.

27. Supine Lateral Dumbbell Raise

The athlete begins in a supine position on a bench or mat holding the dumbbells vertically above his head with his arms almost fully extended and his palms facing one another. He lowers the dumbbells, sideward to shoulder level and returns to the starting position. His elbows are slightly flexed in order to reduce strain on the elbow and shoulder joints (*Figure 1-31*).

28. Standing Dumbbell Swing

The athlete begins in a standing position with one dumbbell held in both hands, palms facing one another, arms extended overhead. Holding his arms extended, he swings the dumbbell downward between his legs as he flexes his hips and returns to the starting position (*Figure 1-32*).

Figure 1-31 **Figure 1-32**

29. Good Morning Exercise

The athlete begins in a standing position with his feet apart, knees locked, the bar behind his shoulders and holding the bar near the collars with a front grip. A towel placed between the bar and his neck will reduce chafing. He flexes his hips until his trunk is parallel to the floor and returns to the starting position (*Figure 1-33*).

Figure 1-33

30. Sit-Up

The athlete begins in a supine position on an inclined board with his feet hooked under the belt. His knees should be slightly bent. He holds a weight (plate, dumbbell or barbell) behind his neck. He sits up to bring his elbows to his knees and returns to the starting position (*Figure 1-34*).

Figure 1-34

31. Neck Flexor

The athlete sits in a chair with his trunk inclined forward and with a head harness on his head to which a weight is attached. He brings his head forward to touch his chin to his chest and extends his head backward as far as his flexibility will allow.

2

EXERCISES WITH
THE ISOMETRIC BELT

The author has designed a series of isometric exercises in which a web belt 1-3/4 inches wide by eighteen feet long is utilized. The belt is stabilized against body parts or objects. A considerably greater variety of exercises are possible than can be done with barbells and dumbbells. There is also a considerable saving in both time and money. The cost of the belt is insignificant in comparison to the cost of a barbell set or universal gym. The same results can be achieved in a twenty-five minute session with the isometric belt as can in a two hour session with barbells.

There is, however, the disadvantage that with the isometric belt there is no "built-in" motivation as there is with barbells. When using barbells the athlete knows how much force he is exerting and is motivated to improve his performance. The author has used the isometric belt in exercise programs for groups ranging in age from six to forty years. Young children need close supervision and manual correction of belt and body positions during the first several sessions. The reader is urged to follow the instructions very meticulously.

GENERAL INSTRUCTIONS

Following are general instructions and suggestions for use of the Isometric Belt:

1. It is of utmost importance that the athlete push or pull against the belt with maximum force. This maximal contraction is held for six seconds. Many people have never experienced a maximal contraction and consequently may believe they are contracting maximally when in actuality they are not. They must *learn* to make a maximal contraction. Some may be lazy. These the coach or physical educator must motivate. He must utilize every motivational device he can. This can include playing recorded march music, setting a good example, verbal urging, and rewards for improvement.

2. For maximal results, as many exercises as possible should be performed two or three times, each time at a different degree of flexion of the involved joint, in order to involve all the muscle fibers maximally. For example, the military press should be done with the forearms at a 45 degree angle to the upper arms, then at a 90 degree angle, and finally with the forearms at a 130 degree angle to the upper arms.

3. During the contraction, the person should maintain uniform intrathoracic pressure by means of a controlled exhalation making an f-f-f-f-f or s-s-s-s-s sound as he exhales air through closed teeth or lips. This procedure will prevent fluctuations in blood pressure.

4. Accurate adjustments in the length of the belt must be made before beginning each exercise in order to position the body segments properly. This will insure that only those muscles which the particular exercise is intended to utilize will be involved in the exercise. For example, in the "shoulder shrug" the belt must be taut while standing on the lower loop with the upper loop held in the hands while the arms, hips and knees are fully extended. If the loop is too long it will become necessary to bend the arms which will cause the arm flexors as well as the trapezius and other shoulder elevators to become involved. If the loop is too short, it will become necessary to flex the hips which will cause the back and hip extensors to become involved. As in body building with weights, each exercise is designed to develop specific muscle groups.

5. When time is limited, exercises should be carefully selected in order to accomplish the desired objectives. The typical conditioning period is thirty minutes in length. All of the isometric exercises described here cannot be completed in that amount of time. For this reason, the instructor may find it advisable to select those isometric exercises which involve the largest muscle groups such as the squat, bent over rowing exercise, dead lift, and rowers' exercise if the exercise session is to be completed in thirty minutes. In other situations, the coach or physical educator might wish to develop the specific muscle groups which are principally involved in the activity being taught. Exercises should then be selected to accomplish the specific objectives.

6. To expedite the exercise session it would be well to present the exercises in such an order that those exercises which require a long loop be presented first and then exercises be presented which require progressively smaller loops. Further, all exercises done standing should be done first, then the sitting exercises, then those done in a lying position and finally those done with a partner or a group. However, exercises involving the same muscle group should not succeed one another.

EXERCISES FOR THE ARMS AND SHOULDER GIRDLE

1. Military Press

The athlete stands on the lower loop of the belt. The straps should run up along the sides of his body, and outside his arms. He grasps the upper loop above his head with his palms forward. His elbows should be flexed. He endeavors to extend his arms directly upward with a maximum force for 6 seconds at each of 3 different degrees of arm flexion. The first contraction should be done with the elbows flexed to a 45 degree angle, the second with them flexed to a 90 degree angle, and the third with the elbows flexed to a 135 degree angle. Adjustments of the belt are made unnecessary by moving the feet closer together or farther apart (*Figures 2-1, 2-2, 2-3*).

2. Press Behind Neck

The athlete stands on the lower loop of a belt. The straps should run up along the side of his body and behind his arms. He grasps the belt with his palms forward and pushes directly upward behind his head. His head should be forward. His elbows should be pointing

Figure 2-1   Figure 2-2   Figure 2-3

Figure 2-4   Figure 2-5   Figure 2-6

sideward. His upper arms should be at an angle to his trunk. His forearms should be at an angle to the upper arms. He should do one maximal contraction for 6 seconds at each of 3 different degrees of flexion of the elbow joint as for the military press. To, in effect, shorten the belt, the feet are moved further apart (*Figures 2-4, 2-5, 2-6*).

3. Supine Press

The athlete begins by lying on the floor in a supine position with the belt around the upper chest and shoulders. He grasps the belt at such a point that his forearms are perpendicular to the floor and at right angles to his upper arms. The belt will be outside the arms. He endeavors to extend the arms directly upward for a maximal contraction of 6 seconds at each of 2 different degrees of arm extension. The first contraction should be done with the elbows flexed to a 90 degree angle and the second contraction with the elbows almost fully extended. (*Figure 2-7*).

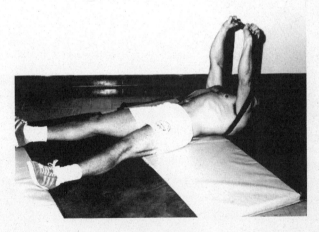

Figure 2-7

4. Arm Depressor

The athlete passes the belt behind his neck and over the front of his shoulders. He reaches between the belt and his body at waist height to grasp the belt at such a position that his elbows will be flexed. He pushes directly downward for a maximal contraction for 6 seconds at each of 3 different degrees of arm flexion. He should make one contraction with his elbows flexed to a 135 degree angle, another at a 90 degree angle, and a third at a 45 degree angle (*Figure 2-8*).

Figure 2-8

5. Front Curl

The athlete stands on the lower loop of the belt and grasps the upper loop of the belt with the palms up at such a position that his elbows are alongside the hips and his forearms at an angle to his upper arms. He endeavors to flex his arms for a maximal contraction for 6 seconds at each of 3 different degrees of elbow flexion. The first contraction should be done with the elbows flexed to a 135 degree angle; the second with them flexed to a 90 degree angle; and the third with them flexed to a 45 degree angle. The feet are moved closer together to lengthen the belt for each succeeding contraction (*Figures 2-9, 2-10, 2-11*).

6. Reverse Curl

The athlete stands on the lower loop of the belt. He reaches around the front of the upper loop of the belt, inserts his hands between the straps and twists his hands counterclockwise to grasp the belt with the palms down. There will be a loop of belt over his hands and wrists. His elbows should be held alongside his hips throughout the exercise.

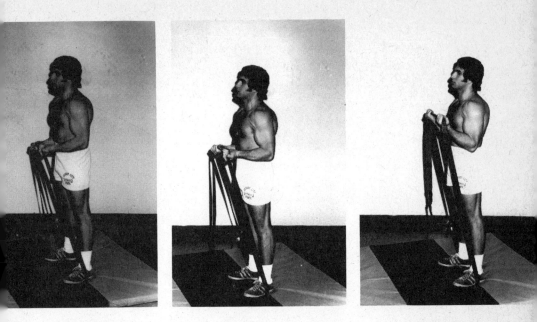

Figure 2-9

Figure 2-10

Figure 2-11

Figure 2-12

Figure 2-13

Figure 2-14

He endeavors to flex his arms at each of three different degrees of elbow flexion. The first contraction should be done with the elbows flexed to a 135 degree angle, the second with them flexed to a 90 degree angle, and the third with them flexed to a 45 degree angle. The feet are moved closer together for each succeeding contraction (*Figures 2-12, 2-13, 2-14*).

7. Standing Pull Up

The athlete begins by standing on the belt with his knees and hips fully extended. He grasps the belt in front of his body with elbows flexed and pointed sideward. He pulls directly upward by attempting to flex the arms for maximal contractions of 6 seconds at each of 3 different degrees of elbow flexion; i.e., at 135, 90 and 45 degrees of elbow flexion (*Figure 2-15*).

Figure 2-15

8. Forward Extended Arm Depressor

The upper loop of the belt is placed over a door or similar stable object. The athlete grasps the lower loop with both hands. He pushes downward with both hands while holding the arms in an extended position. He should do 3 maximal contractions of 6 seconds duration at each of 3 different levels of arm elevation. The first contraction should be done with the extended arms forming a 135 degree angle with the trunk; the second with arms forming a right angle with the trunk; and the third with them forming a 45 degree angle with the trunk.

9. Forward Extended Arm Elevator

The athlete begins by standing on the loop of the belt. He grasps the upper loop with both hands and pulls upward with the arms in an extended position and elevated in front of the body. He does 3 maximal contractions for 6 seconds each at 3 different degrees of arm elevation. The first contraction should be done with the arms 45 degrees from the vertical, the second 90 degrees from the vertical and the third with them 135 degrees from the vertical (*Figures 2-16, 2-17, 2-18*).

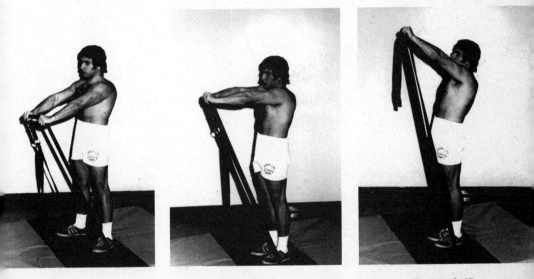

| Figure 2-16 | Figure 2-17 | Figure 2-18 |

10. Sideward Extended Arm Depressor

The upper loop of the belt is placed over a door or similar stable object at a similar height. The athlete grasps the lower loop with the right hand with her right arm extended sideward. She endeavors to push the extended arm downward. The same exercise should be done for the muscles of the left shoulder. Three maximal contractions for each arm at each of 3 different degrees (45, 90 and 135 from the vertical) of arm elevation should be done (*Figure 2-19*).

Figure 2-19

11. Sideward Extended Arm Elevator

The athlete stands on the lower loop of the belt with the heel of the right foot. He grasps the upper loop with the right hand with the right arm extended sideward. With the right arm extended, he endeavors to pull upward as hard as he is able. The same exercise for the muscles of the left shoulder should be done. Three maximal contractions of 6 seconds for each arm at each of 3 different degrees of arm elevation should be done. One contraction with the arm at a 45 degree angle to the trunk, another with the arm at a 90 degree angle to the trunk, and a third with the arm at a 135 degree angle to the trunk should be done.

Figure 2-20   **Figure 2-21**   **Figure 2-22**

The exercise may be done with the palms turned upward or downward or both for a total of 12 contractions (*Figures 2-20, 2-21, 2-22*).

SPECIAL EXERCISES

12. Golfer's Exercise

The belt is wrapped around the lower end of a golf club or wand. The athlete stands on the belt with both feet in a normal stance. He grasps the handle of the club or wand and endeavors to swing. One maximal contraction for 6 seconds should be done.

13. Bowler's Exercise

The athlete assumes the position of the bowler in each of 3 stages of delivery of the ball. The left leg should be forward with the left knee bent. The right leg should be extended well to the rear. The trunk should be vertical and rotating counterclockwise. The student stands on the lower loop with his right leg. He grasps the upper loop with the right hand. He pulls with the arm and the body as he pushes with the right leg. He should do one maximal contraction for 6 seconds at each of 3 different stages of delivery (*Figure 2-23*).

Figure 2-23

14. Javelin Thrower's Exercise

The athlete takes the position of the javelin thrower in the initial stage of the throw; that is, with the left leg forward, the right foot about

18 inches behind the left foot, the trunk arched slightly backward and rotated clockwise. The right elbow is pointed in the direction of the throw. He grasps one loop of the belt in the left hand. He passes the belt outside the left shoulder, behind the back, and outside the right shoulder to grasp the other loop in the right hand. The belt may also be stabilized by hooking one end over some item as illustrated. He pulls as hard as he is able for 6 seconds. He should do a total of 3 maximal contractions of 6 seconds each with each arm at different stages of the throw. Note: The illustrations show a left handed thrower (*Figures 2-24, 2-25, 2-26*).

Figure 2-24   Figure 2-25   Figure 2-26

15. Shot Putter's Exercise

The athlete assumes the position of the shot putter in the initial stage of the throw. He hooks the left thumb in one loop of the belt. He passes the belt outside the left shoulder, behind the back, and outside the right shoulder. He places the other loop across the palm of the right hand. An alternate method for stabilizing the belt is to hook one loop over some object on the wall. With the elbow behind the hand, he pushes upward and outward at a 45 degree angle to the floor. He should do 3 maximal contractions at each of 3 different stages in the put. To assure a balanced and symmetrical body development, he should do 3 maximal contractions for 6 seconds each with the left arm as though shot putting with the left hand. The athlete in the illustration is left handed (*Figures 2-27, 2-28, 2-29*).

| Figure 2-27 | Figure 2-28 | Figure 2-29 |

16. Pole Vaulter's Exercise

The athlete passes both straps of the belt behind the lower part of the neck. She grasps the two pieces hanging down in front of her chest and pulls downward with the elbows elevated and flexed. She should do 3 maximal contractions for 6 seconds each at 3 different degrees of elbow flexion; i.e., with the elbows flexed to 135, 90, and 45 degrees (*Figure 2-30*).

Figure 2-30

17. Swimmer's Exercise

The athlete places one loop of the belt over a doorknob or similar stable object at a comparable height. Facing the belt, she bends forward at the hips so that her trunk is parallel to the floor. She grasps the lower loop in the left hand, and with the left arm at about a 45 degree angle to the floor and the elbow bent about 30 degrees, she pulls downward and backward. The same exercise is done for the right arm.

Butterfly swimmers should do both arms simultaneously. A maximal contraction for 6 seconds at this position, one with the arm (or arms) vertical and then another with the arm (or arms) 10 degrees behind the vertical should be done (*Figures 2-31 and 2-32*).

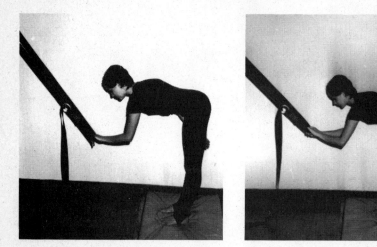

| Figure 2-31 | Figure 2-32 |

18. Rower's Exercise

The athlete sits on the floor with his knees flexed so that the shin bones form approximately a 135 degree angle with the thigh bones. He places his feet inside the lower loop. The belt should pass over the heels. The straps should pass along the outside of the legs. The upper loop should pass around the outside of and behind the thighs. The athlete reaches around the outside of the belt and over the top of it and twists his wrists so that a section of the belt passes over the wrists. He pulls backward with the arms, shoulders, and back as he endeavors to extend the legs for one maximal contraction of 6 seconds (*Figure 2-33*).

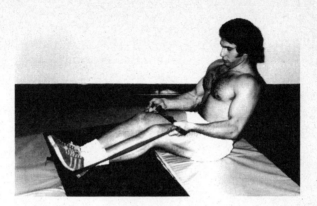

Figure 2-33

19. Pull Over

The athletes are paired. One partner assumes a supine position with arms on the floor extended overhead. He grasps the belt with his palms up. His partner stands on the end of the belt. The belt should be stretched out. The supine athlete endeavors to pull his extended arms upward for 3 maximal contractions of 6 seconds each. The first contraction should be with the extended arms just above the floor, the second with the arms forming a 30 degree angle with the floor, and the third with the arms at a 50 degree angle to the floor (*Figure 2-34*).

Figure 2-34

EXERCISES FOR THE WRISTS AND HANDS

20. Wrist and Forearm Exercise

The athlete starts in a squatting position with the belt under his feet. He grasps the belt with palms up and with his forearms resting along his thighs. He endeavors to flex his wrists for one maximal contraction of 6 seconds. He should avoid attempting to flex his elbows. He should do one contraction with the palms turned downward and one with the palms turned upward (*Figures 2-35 and 2-36*).

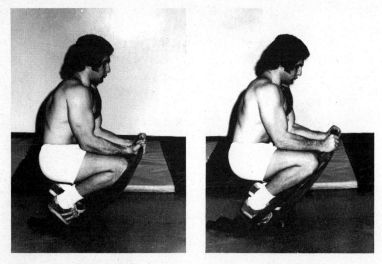

Figure 2-35   Figure 2-36

EXERCISES FOR THE TRUNK AND NECK

21. Forward Push (Neck)

The athlete places the belt against his forehead and endeavors to push his head forward against the resistance offered by the arms through the belt for a maximal contraction for 6 seconds (*Figure 2-37*).

22. Backward Push (Neck)

The athlete places the belt against the back of his head and endeavors to push his head backward against the resistance offered by the arms through the belt for a maximal contraction for 6 seconds (*Figure 2-38*).

Figure 2-37

Figure 2-38

23. Sideward Push (Neck)

The athlete places the belt against the side of his head and endeavors to tilt his head sideward against the resistance offered by the arms through the belt for a maximal contraction for 6 seconds. He should do one contraction to each side (*Figure 2-39*).

24. Head Turn (Neck)

The athlete places the belt almost completely around his head and across his forehead. He endeavors to turn his head as though trying to look sideward over the shoulder against the resistance offered by the arms through the belt. He should do one contraction for 6 seconds to each side (*Figure 2-40*).

Figure 2-39

Figure 2-40

25. Front Shoulder Shrug

The athlete stands with his heels on the belt and with his hips, knees and arms fully extended. He grasps the belt with his palms toward the body and pulls upward by elevating the shoulders. The arms should remain extended throughout the exercise. This exercise will develop principally the trapezius muscles which will give the neck the slope that identifies the strong man. He should do one maximal contraction for 6 seconds (*Figure 2-41*).

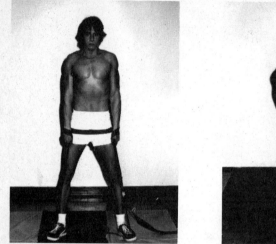   

Figure 2-41   **Figure 2-42**

26. Back Shoulder Shrug

The athlete stands with his heels on the belt and the belt behind his body. His body is erect and his arms, hips and knees are fully extended. He grasps the belt behind his hips with the palms facing rearward. He pulls upward by endeavoring to elevate his shoulders for one maximal contraction of 6 seconds. There should be no bending of the arms during the exercise. Only the shoulders should be elevated (*Figure 2-42*).

27. Chest Pull

The athlete grasps the belt with both hands in front of his chin. His elbows are elevated. His hands should be about 6 inches apart. It will be helpful if he wraps the belt around his hands. He tries to pull outward for a maximal contraction of 6 seconds at each of two different spacings of the hands (*Figure 2-43*).

Figure 2-43   **Figure 2-44**

28. Chest Push

The athlete passes both straps of the belt behind his back and around the outside of his shoulders. He reaches under the two loops of the belt to grasp them with the palms turned downward and with the hands 2 to 6 inches apart. He endeavors to push his hands toward each other for 2 maximal contractions of 6 seconds at each of two different spacings of the hands (*Figure 2-44*).

29. Supine Extended Arm Elevator

The athlete begins by lying on the floor in a supine position with the belt passed around his hips. His hands are at shoulder width and his arms are at an angle to the floor. He endeavors to pull the extended arms upward for a maximal contraction of 6 seconds at each of 2 different degrees of shoulder elevation. The first contraction should be done with the extended arms at a 30 degree angle to the floor, the second with the arms at a 60 degree angle to the floor (*Figure 2-45*).

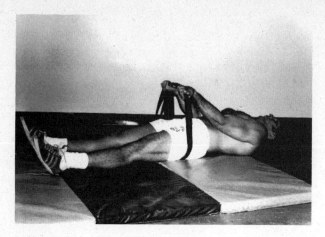

Figure 2-45

30. Bent Over Rowing Exercise

The athlete stands with his heels on the lower loop of the belt. He keeps his legs fully extended and bends forward at the hips until his trunk is almost parallel to the floor. He places his hands inside the loop and then twists them around to loop the belt around his wrists. He pulls upward by trying to flex his arms for 3 maximal contractions of 6 seconds each at 3 different degrees of elbow flexion. In each contraction the back should be almost parallel to the floor, but the elbows should be flexed to 135, 90 and 45 degree angles in the three contractions (*Figure 2-46*).

Figure 2-46

31. Dead Lift

The athlete stands with his heels on the lower loop of the belt. He bends forward until his hips are flexed between a 170 and a 135 degree angle. His arms and legs should be held fully extended throughout the exercise. Because of the great amount of force generated, the belt should be wrapped around the wrists. The athlete endeavors to come to the erect position by pulling with the muscles of the back. He should do maximal contractions of 6 seconds duration at each of 2 different degrees of hip flexion. The first contraction should be done with the trunk forming a 135 degree angle with the legs and the second with the trunk forming about a 170 degree angle with the legs (*Figure 2-47*).

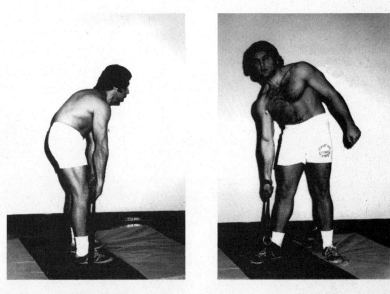

Figure 2-47   **Figure 2-48**

32. Suitcase Lift

The athlete stands on the lower loop of the belt with his right foot. He places his right hand into the upper loop and twists his hand half-way around to grasp both sides of the belt. His arm should be fully extended. He endeavors to pull directly sideward as though lifting a very heavy suitcase. He should do the exercise to each side for a maximal contraction of 6 seconds duration (*Figure 2-48*).

EXERCISES FOR THE LEGS AND FEET

33. Squat

The athlete stands with his heels on the belt. He bends both knees to approximately a 130 degree angle. He passes the belt along the outside of his legs and up over the bony portion of his hips. He should keep his trunk as nearly vertical as possible by arching his lower back. He endeavors to extend his legs for two maximal contractions of 6 seconds. The first contraction should be done with the knee joints at approximately a 130 degree angle and the second with the knees at approximately a 155 degree angle. The knees should not be flexed to less than a 120 degree angle (*Figure 2-49*).

Figure 2-49

Figure 2-50

34. Sitting Leg Extensor

The athlete sits on the floor with the knees flexed so that the thighs are at a 135 degree angle to the lower legs. He passes the belt behind his hips over the bony part, along the side of his legs and in front of his heels. He endeavors to extend his knees for one maximal contraction of 6 seconds (*Figure 2-50*).

35. Prone Leg Extensor

The athlete lies on his abdomen with his knees bent. The belt should pass over his insteps, along his back, over his shoulders and be held in his hands in front of his neck. He should endeavor to extend his legs for one maximal contraction of 6 seconds (*Figure 2-51*).

Figure 2-51

36. Supine Hip Flexor

The athlete assumes a supine position. He places his left foot in the lower loop with the belt against the bottom of the foot. He next places the right foot inside the upper loop with the belt against the instep. He maintains the left leg in a fully extended position as he endeavors to more fully flex the right hip and knee (bring the right knee upward toward his head). He reverses the positions of the legs to develop the hip and knee flexors of the left hip. He should do one maximal contraction of 6 seconds duration for each leg (*Figure 2-52*).

Figure 2-52

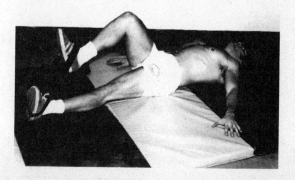

37. Sitting Leg Abductor

The athlete assumes a sitting position. He places both feet inside the belt so that the belt runs outside his ankles. He endeavors to abduct (pull apart) the extended legs for maximal contractions of 6 seconds duration at each of three different degrees of leg abduction; that is, with the feet about one, two and three feet apart (*Figure 2-53*).

38. Sitting Leg Adductor

The athlete passes one loop of the belt around the inside of the right knee. Someone may hold the other loop of the belt, it may be hooked around a stable object or it may be held with the right hand against the floor to the right side of the body. The athlete should endeavor to adduct (pull toward the mid-line of the body) the extended leg. The same exercise should be done for the left leg. Two maximal contractions of 6 seconds duration each at two different degrees of adduction for each leg should be done (*Figure 2-54*).

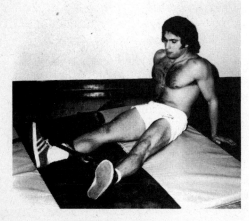   

Figure 2-53   **Figure 2-54**

39. Side Leg Flexor

The athlete lies on his left side with his left leg extended forward and his right leg extended backward with the right knee slightly bent. The belt should pass over the ankle of the left foot and over the heel of the right foot. He endeavors to flex the right knee for one maximal contraction of 6 seconds. Having done this, he reverses the procedure

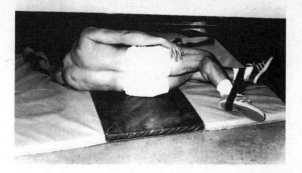

Figure 2-55

by turning onto his right side to do the exercise for the "hamstrings" (knee flexors) of the left leg (*Figure 2-55*).

40. Side Leg Extensor

The athlete begins by lying on his left side with his left leg forward and slightly flexed, his right leg backward and extended, his left arm along the floor overhead, and his right hand on the floor. The belt should be passed around his left ankle and halfway over his right heel. He should endeavor to pull his extended right leg backward against the resistance of the belt for one maximal contraction for 6 seconds duration. One contraction should also be done while lying on the right side for the left leg. This develops primarily the gluteals (*Figure 2-56*).

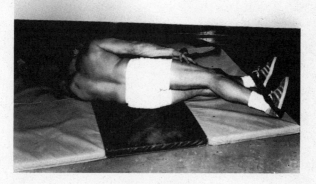

Figure 2-56

41. Sitting Leg Raiser

Starting in a sitting position on the floor, the athlete inserts both legs into the loop of the belt so that the belt is at ankle level of both legs. He endeavors to lift the extended right leg for one maximal contraction of 6 seconds as illustrated. He then does the same exercise for the hip flexors of the left leg (*Figure 2-57*).

42. Rise on Toes

The athlete stands on the lower loop with the balls of both feet. He brings the two straps up in front of his chest and places the upper loop behind the lower part of his neck. It is important that the belt be adjusted so that it will be taut and yet permit the student to stand erect and in good posture with the hips and knees fully extended, heels down. The athlete attempts to rise up on his toes against the resistance offered by the belt for one maximal contraction of 6 seconds duration. He should avoid hunching the shoulders (*Figure 2-58*).

Figure 2-57   Figure 2-58

43. Sitting Plantar Flexor

The athlete starts in a sitting position with both legs extended. The belt should pass behind his hips (over the bony part) alongside his legs and over the balls of the feet. The feet should be dorsiflexcd. The athlete attempts to plantar flex (point the toes) the feet against the resistance of the belt for one maximal contraction of 6 seconds (*Figure 2-59*).

Figure 2-59

44. Sitting Dorsal Flexor

The athlete starts in a sitting position with his legs extended. He places both feet inside the upper loop. Another athlete may hold the lower loop or it may be hooked over a stable object. He endeavors to dorsiflex the feet (pull the feet toward his face). Having neither partner nor a stable object, the athlete can achieve the same result by placing the left foot in the lower loop so that the belt passes across the bottom of the foot and placing the right foot in the upper loop so that the belt passes across his instep. He may also team-up with a partner as illustrated. With the right leg bent and the left extended, he then endeavors to dorsal flex the right foot. He should do one maximal contraction for 6 seconds for each foot (*Figure 2-60*).

Figure 2-60

45. Sitting Foot Adductor

The athlete starts in a sitting position on the floor with his legs straddled. He inserts the right foot into the lower loop so that the belt passes over the inside of the big toe. He holds the upper loop in his right hand with the right arm extended and at a 45 degree angle to the body. The belt may also be held by a partner or hooked to a stable object. He endeavors to bend the foot directly inward (adduction) using the heel as a fulcrum. He should do the same exercise for the left foot. One maximal contraction for each foot of 6 seconds duration should be done (*Figure 2-61*).

Figure 2-61   **Figure 2-62**

46. Sitting Foot Abductor

The athlete starts in a sitting position on the floor with his legs straddled. He inserts both feet into the loop so that the belt passes over the outside of the little toes. He endeavors to bend the feet outward, using the heels as fulcra. One maximal contraction of 6 seconds duration should be done (*Figure 2-62*).

INSTRUCTIONS FOR USE OF ISOMETRIC BELTS

Class or Team

It is as simple to lead a group of ten to one hundred athletes in doing isometric exercises with the Isometric Belt as it is for each person to do the exercise individually. The most effective class formation is with athletes in a circle or in two or more concentric circles. The athletes should face the center of the circle where the coach will stand to explain and to demonstrate. In this formation, all athletes will be most easily able to see and to hear the coach. By taking a few steps the coach can reach any athlete to give manual and individual instruction and motivation. The interval between athletes should be approximately five feet. One or two of the athletes can be assigned the task of distributing the belts to other athletes while the coach takes roll or makes necessary announcements.

At the initial meeting the coach demonstrates each exercise three times facing a different direction each time to insure that all athletes see the procedures to be followed. The exercise should be named each time. At the second meeting, one demonstration will very likely suffice. After a few meetings, it will become necessary that the coach merely name the exercise. During the initial demonstrations, hand, belt, and body positions should be described verbally as well as demonstrated. The degree of flexion should be indicated. In the military press for example, the coach could say: "Upper arms at a right angle to the trunk, forearms at a 45 degree angle to the upper arms, elbows pointed forward, palms forward, knees and hips fully extended."

To aid athletes in developing their sense of time, the instructor could count off the seconds during the contraction by counting. "One-two-three," etc. This procedure makes it mandatory that athletes begin and end together. Since some students will require more time than others to adjust their belt, some time will be lost due to having to wait for the slow ones. After several class meetings, athletes will learn the sequence of the exercises (if the sequence followed is always the same). When this stage has been reached, each athlete can count for himself and proceed to the next exercise when he is ready. When each athlete begins the next exercise when he is ready, it will not be necessary for members to wait for the slowest athlete and time will be saved.

In most exercises, athletes will stabilize the belt against their own body segments. These exercises have been described. However, in a few exercises they should work in pairs or as a class.

PROCEDURE FOR CONSTRUCTION OF THE ISOMETRIC BELT

The Isometric Belt can be made quite easily if the necessary materials and equipment can be secured. A strong and heavy but soft and flexible web or cable belt 1-3/4 inches in width, 18 feet long, and strong enough to withstand a strain of 2,500 pounds, two steel rings 2-1/2 inches in diameter, and heavy thread are needed for each belt. A shoemaker's sewing machine or one of the type used to repair athletic equipment is needed to sew the rings to the belt. The belting must be soft and flexible enough that it may be wrapped around the hands or wrists and not cut into the skin while pulling on the belt with several hundred pounds of force as will be done in the "dead lift" or "rowing exercise."

The webbing is most difficult to locate. It may be found at local harness shops or surplus centers. The rings can be found in some local hardware stores. A local shoemaker or athletic equipment repair shop can sew the rings to the belt.

One end of the belt is passed through the center of the two rings, folded back about four inches of its length and sewn with heavy thread as illustrated: The belt is adjusted for length by passing the free end through the center of the two rings, doubling it back over the top of the uppermost ring, and passing it between the two rings (*Figures 2-63 and 2-64*). The belt may be shortened by pulling on the outside strap. It may be lengthened by pulling on the inside strap while holding the rings apart with the fingers and thumb of one hand.

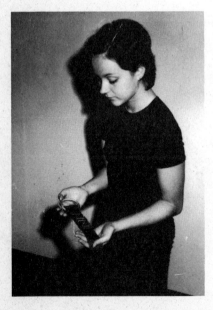

Figure 2-63

Figure 2-64

3

ISOMETRIC EXERCISES WITH A BEACH TOWEL, PARTNER AND WITHOUT EQUIPMENT

ISOMETRIC EXERCISES WITH A TOWEL

Many isometric exercises can be done with an ordinary beach towel. The beach towel should be as large as possible and in good condition. Team members could do these exercises after practice in the locker room. The energy cost of isometric exercises is quite low; consequently, they could be utilized during the competitive season to sustain strength and power which normally decline as the season progresses.

As in doing the isometric exercises with a belt, the athlete should exhale with an f-f-f-f-f or s-s-s-s-s sound during the contraction.

EXERCISES FOR THE ARMS AND SHOULDER GIRDLE

1. Military Press

The athlete places the middle of the towel behind his back with both ends running under his arms and upward in front of his shoulders. He grasps the ends and pushes directly upward with a maximal contraction for six seconds at each of three different degrees of elbow flexion—45°, 90°, and 135° of flexion at the elbow. To increase the angle at the elbow joint, the athlete grasps the towel nearer the ends (*Figure 3-1*).

Figure 3-1

2. Press Behind Neck

This exercise is done in the same manner as the military press except that the thrust is upward behind the head rather than upward in front of the head.

3. Supine Press

The athlete begins in a supine position with the center of the towel under his upper back and the ends running upward outside his arms to his hands. He pushes directly upward for three maximal contractions—one with elbows flexed at 45°, one at 90° and one at 135° (*Figure 3-2*).

Figure 3-2

4. Arm Depressor

The athlete places the center of the towel behind his neck with the ends running downward in front of his chest. He is in a standing position. He grasps the ends of the towel and pushes directly downward with a maximal contraction at each of three different degrees of elbow flexion—45°, 90°, and 135° (*Figure 3-3*).

Figure 3-3

5. Front Curl

The athlete is seated on a chair, bench or table. He places the center of the towel behind his knees and grasps the ends with palms up and with the forearms at 135° to his upper arms. His elbows are alongside his hips. His trunk is perpendicular to the floor. He endeavors to flex his elbows for a maximal contraction for six seconds. He does a six second maximal contraction at 45° and at 90° of elbow flexion (*Figure 3-4*).

6. Reverse Curl

This exercise is done in the same manner as the front curl except the ends of the towel are wrapped around the hands once and the palms are turned downward. The elbows should be pressed against the sides throughout the exercise (*Figure 3-5*).

Figure 3-4

Figure 3-5

7. Standing Pull-Up

The athlete stands erect on the center of the towel and wraps the ends around his hands so that his elbows are flexed and pointed sideward. He pulls directly upward by attempting to flex his arms for maximal contractions of six seconds at each of two different degrees of elbow flexion; i.e., at 135° and 90° (*Figure 3-6*).

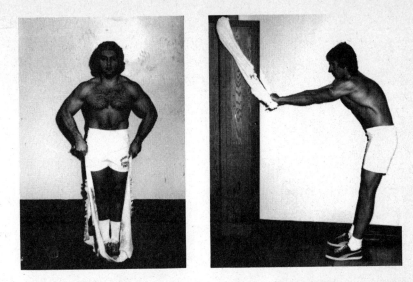

Figure 3-6   **Figure 3-7**

8. Forward Extended Arm Depressor

The athlete places the center of the towel over a horizontal bar, pipe or other object, wraps an end of the towel around each hand and in a standing position with arms extended forward endeavors to push directly downward. He should do three maximal contractions of six seconds duration—one with his arms at 135° to his trunk, one with his arms at 90° to his trunk (arms horizontal) and one with his arms at 45° to his body (*Figure 3-7*).

9. Sideward Extended Arm Depressor

The towel is placed in the same position as in the preceding exercise; however, the athlete stands with his side toward the towel and grasps the towel with one hand with his arm extended sideward. He endeavors to bring his extended arm downward against the resistance of the towel for a maximal contraction of six seconds duration. He should do three contractions with each arm with the arm at 135°, 90° and 45° to the trunk (*Figure 3-8*).

10. Forward Extended Arm Elevator

The athlete sits on a chair, bench or table. He places the center of the towel behind his knees and grasps one end in each hand. With arms

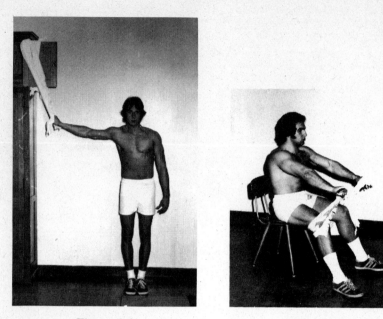

Figure 3-8   Figure 3-9

extended and at an angle to his trunk, he pulls his extended arms upward against the resistance offered by the towel for a maximal contraction of six seconds with his arms at 45° and at 90° angles to his trunk (*Figure 3-9*).

11. Sideward Extended Arm Elevator

The athlete is standing erect with his left foot on the lower end of the towel. He grasps the towel at such a height that his extended left arm is at a 45° angle to his trunk and pulls upward with his palm turned downward and his arm extended for a maximal contraction for six seconds. He does the same with his palm turned upward. He does one contraction with the extended arm at 90° to the trunk with his palm turned upward and another with the palm turned downward. He then does the four contractions with his right arm. Finally, he does two contractions with each arm, one with palm turned upward and one with palm turned downward, with the extended arm at 135° to the trunk. These latter contractions are done while seated on a chair or bench and holding the end of the towel down with the foot on the side of the arm being exercised (*Figure 3-10*).

Figure 3-10

12. Pole Vaulter's Exercise

The athlete places the towel behind his neck with the two ends hanging in front of his chest. He grasps the towel in front of his chest with his elbows flexed to 45° and elevated and makes a maximal six second contraction. He makes two additional contractions grasping the towel at lower points so that his elbows form 90° and 135° angles (*Figure 3-11*).

Figure 3-11

13. Swimmer's Exercise

The athlete places the middle of the towel over a pipe, bar, or vertical ladder (stall bars) or other substantially anchored object at between chest and waist height. He grasps the end of the towel with palm turned downward, flexes his hips until his trunk is parallel to the floor and with his elbow flexed about 30° and his arm at 135° to his trunk and pulls downward and backward for a maximal contraction for six seconds. He does additional contractions with his arm at 90° and at 45° to the trunk. Finally, he does the three contractions with his other arm at 135°, 90°, and 45° to the trunk (*Figure 3-12*).

Butterfly swimmers do the same contractions in the same manner except that they use both arms simultaneously.

Figure 3-12

EXERCISES FOR THE LEGS AND FEET

14. Sitting Leg Extensor

The athlete is in a sitting position on the floor with his knees flexed to about 135°. He places the center of the towel outside his heels and wraps one end of the towel around each hand so that the towel is taut when his arms are fully extended. He endeavors to extend his legs against the resistance of the towel for a maximal contraction of six seconds (*Figure 3-13*).

15. Sitting Plantar Flexor

The athlete is seated on the floor with his legs fully extended. He places the center of the beach towel over the balls of his feet, wraps

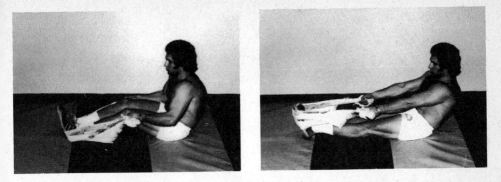

Figure 3-13   **Figure 3-14**

one end of the towel around each hand so that the towel is taut when his arms are fully extended. He endeavors to point his toes (plantar flex his feet) against the resistance of the towel for a maximal contraction of six seconds (*Figure 3-14*).

16. Prone Leg Extensor

The athlete is lying on his abdomen. He places the center of the beach towel on his insteps and wraps one end of the towel around each hand so that the towel is taut when his arms are extended along his sides and his knees are flexed to a 90° angle. He endeavors to extend his knees for a maximal contraction for six seconds (*Figure 3-15*).

Figure 3-15

17. Supine Hip Flexor

The athlete begins in a supine position. The ends of the beach towel have been tied in a square knot so that the towel forms a loop.

The left heel and the right instep are inside the loop. Both legs are extended. The athlete endeavors to lift his leg against the resistance of the towel in a maximal contraction for six seconds. He reverses the position of the legs and does another six second contraction (*Figure 3-16*).

Figure 3-16   Figure 3-17

18. Sitting Leg Abductor

The athlete is in a sitting position on the floor with his legs extended. The ends of the beach towel are tied together with a square knot so that the towel forms a loop. He places his feet inside the loop and endeavors to pull his extended legs apart for a maximal contraction for six seconds (*Figure 3-17*).

19. Sitting Foot Abductor

The athlete is in a sitting position on the floor with his legs extended. The ends of the beach towel are tied in a square knot. He places both feet inside the loop with the towel just below the level of the little toe. Using his heels as fulcrum points, he endeavors to rotate his feet outward against the resistance of the towel in a maximal contraction for six seconds (*Figure 3-18*).

20. Side Leg Flexor

The athlete is lying on his right side with his right leg extended forward and his left leg in line with his body and his left knee slightly flexed. The towel is tied to form a loop and the feet are inside the loop so that the towel passes around both ankles. The athlete endeavors to flex his left knee for a maximal contraction for six seconds. The athlete then does a contraction with the right knee having rolled over to his left side and reversing the procedures (*Figure 3-19*).

Figure 3-18   **Figure 3-19**

21. Side Leg Extensor

The starting and towel positions are the same as in the side leg flexor except that both legs are fully extended. The athlete endeavors to pull the extended upper leg backward (hyperextend the hip joint) in a maximal contraction of six seconds duration. He next rolls over to his opposite side and reverses the procedures to exercise the hip extensors on the opposite side (*Figure 3-20*).

Figure 3-20

22. Sitting Leg Adductor

The athlete is in a sitting position on the floor with both legs extended. The center of the beach towel is passed around the inside of his leg. A partner holds the ends of the towel to offer resistance as the athlete attempts to adduct (pull toward the midline of the body) his leg. The ends of the towel may also be tied in a square knot. The partner then inserts a leg into the loop and they engage in a "tug-of-war." They then exchange positions to exercise the leg adductors of the opposite leg (*Figure 3-21*).

Figure 3-21

23. Sitting Foot Adductor

Two athletes are in a sitting position side by side on the floor with their legs extended and straddled. The ends of the towel are tied in a square knot and the athletes place the foot which is nearest their partner inside the loop with the towel at the level of the little toe. Using the heels as fulcra, they endeavor to adduct the foot (rotate it inward toward the "pigeon toed" position). They then exchange positions to exercise the adductors of the opposite foot. One partner may also hold the towel as illustrated (*Figure 3-22*).

24. Sitting Dorsi Flexor

The athletes are in a sitting position on the floor with their legs extended. They are facing one another with their feet about 24 inches apart. A beach towel with ends tied so that the towel forms a loop is

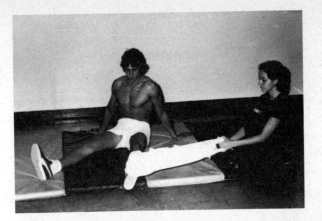

Figure 3-22

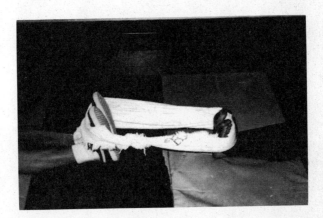

Figure 3-23

placed over the feet of the athletes at the level of the little toe. The athletes engage in a "tug-of-war" as they endeavor to dorsiflex or bring their toes toward their head (*Figure 3-23*).

EXERCISES FOR THE TRUNK AND NECK

25. Chest Pull

The athlete wraps the towel around each hand so that the hands are two to eight inches apart in front of the neck. Holding his elbows up, he endeavors to pull the towel apart for a maximal contraction of six seconds (*Figure 3-24*).

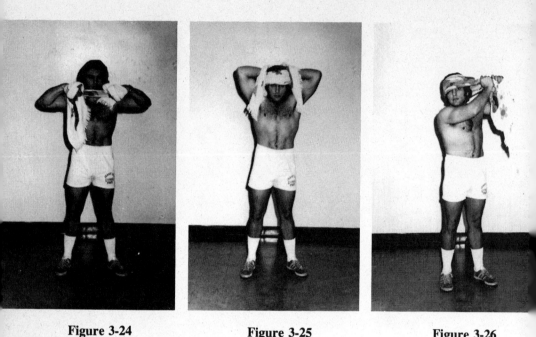

Figure 3-24   **Figure 3-25**   **Figure 3-26**

26. Head Forward Push

The athlete holds the towel against his forehead while he endeavors to push his head forward against the resistance offered by his arms through the towel (*Figure 3-25*).

27. Head Backward Push

The athlete holds the towel against the back of his head and endeavors to push his head backward.

28. Head Sideward Push

The athlete holds the towel against the side of his head and endeavors to push his head toward that side. He does one contraction to each side.

29. Head Turn

The athlete places the towel almost completely around his head and across his forehead. He endeavors to turn his head as though trying to look backward over his shoulder. He does one contraction in each direction (*Figure 3-26*).

30. Supine Extended Arm Elevator

The athlete assumes a lying position on the floor. He passes the towel under his pelvis and wraps one end around each hand. He endeavors to elevate his extended arms against the resistance of the towel for a maximal contraction of six seconds at each of three levels of elevation of the arms (*Figure 3-27*).

Figure 3-27

31. Pull Over

The athlete is lying on the floor with her arms extended above her head and the ends of the towel wrapped around each hand. A partner is holding down the center of the towel. The athlete endeavors to elevate her extended arms against the resistance of the towel for a maximal contraction of six seconds at each of three different levels of elevation of the arms (*Figure 3-28*).

Figure 3-28

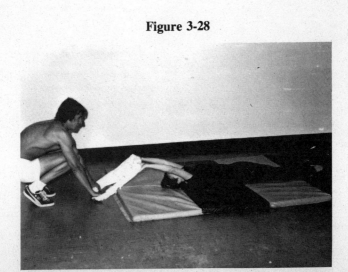

32. Bent Over Rowing Exercise

The athlete is standing on the center of the beach towel with one end of the towel wrapped around each hand. His hips are flexed so that his trunk is parallel to the floor and his elbows are bent. He pulls upward with his arms for a maximal contraction of six seconds (*Figure 3-29*).

33. Dead Lift

The athlete stands on the center of the towel with one end of the towel wrapped around each hand. His arms are fully extended and his hips are flexed to approximately a 135° angle. He endeavors to extend his hips (come to the erect position) against the resistance of the towel for a maximal contraction of six seconds (*Figure 3-30*).

34. Suitcase Lift

The athlete stands on the center of the towel with his right foot, bends his trunk to the right and wraps both ends of the towel around his right hand. With his arm fully extended, he endeavors to pull directly sideward (as though lifting a heavy suitcase). He does a maximal contraction for six seconds on each side (*Figure 3-31*).

Figure 3-29   **Figure 3-30**   **Figure 3-31**

EXERCISES FOR THE WRISTS AND HANDS

35. Wrist Front Curl

The athlete stands on the center of the towel, squats, places his forearms on his thighs with the hands just beyond the knees and wraps an end of the towel around each hand. With his palms facing upward, he endeavors to flex his wrists against the resistance of the towel for a maximal contraction of six seconds. He should avoid flexing his elbows (*Figure 3-32*).

Figure 3-32

36. Wrist Reverse Curl

This exercise is done in exactly the same manner as the wrist front curl except that the palms are turned downward.

ISOMETRIC EXERCISES WITHOUT EQUIPMENT

All of the muscle groups can be developed through utilization of isometric exercises in which no special equipment is required. The athlete can do the exercises in his dorm room or at home making use of the door frame, a chair, desk, or the resistance of a partner.

EXERCISES FOR THE ARMS AND SHOULDERS GIRDLE

37. Extended Arm Elevator

The athlete stands between the door with his arms along the sides of his body and the back of his hands against the door frame. He endeavors to lift his extended arms upward against the door frame for a maximal contraction of six seconds. He also does one contraction with the palms toward the door frame (*Figure 3-33*).

38. Extended Arm Depressor

The athlete stands slightly behind the door with his arms extended overhead and the backs of his hands toward the door frame. He endeavors to depress his extended arms against the resistance of the door frame for a maximal contraction of six seconds. He also does one contraction with his palms toward the door frame (*Figure 3-34*).

Figure 3-33   **Figure 3-34**

39. Flexed Arm Elevator

The athlete stands between the door frame with his arms flexed and his elbows against the frame. He endeavors to lift his flexed arms for a maximal contraction of six seconds (*Figure 3-35*).

40. Flexed Arm Depressor

The athlete stands between the door frame with his arms flexed above his head and his elbows against the door frame. He endeavors to

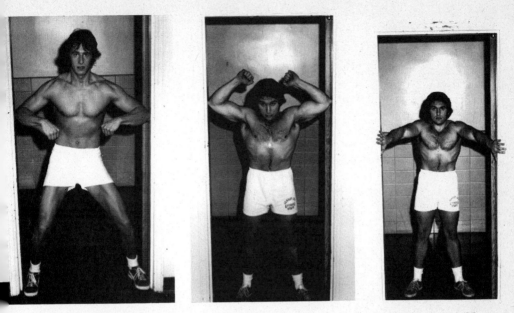

| Figure 3-35 | Figure 3-36 | Figure 3-37 |

depress his flexed arms for a maximal contraction of six seconds (*Figure 3-36*).

41. Forward Extended Arm Sideward Mover

The athlete stands behind the door frame with his arms extended forward and his palms against the frame. He endeavors to pull his extended arms apart for a maximal contraction of six seconds. He also does one contraction with the back of his hands toward the frame (*Figure 3-37*).

42. Arm Extensor

The athlete stands between the door with his back against one side of the frame and his palms against the other side. He endeavors to extend his arms for a maximal contraction of six seconds.

43. Front Curl on a Desk

The athlete is seated on a chair in front of a desk at such a distance that with his elbows at his sides he can place his palms under the edge of the desk. He endeavors to flex his elbows for a maximal contraction of six seconds.

44. Reverse Curl on Desk

This exercise is done in the same manner as the front curl on a desk except that the backs of the hands are against the underside of the edge of the desk.

45. Arm Depressor on Desk

The athlete is seated in a chair in front of a desk. He places his palms on the desk and with arms extended presses downward on the desk for a maximal contraction of six seconds. He also does one contraction with the back of his hands on the desk.

46. Arm Depressor on Chair

The athlete is seated in a chair and places his palms against the front legs of the chair. His arms are extended. He presses his extended arms backward for one maximal contraction of six seconds. He also does one contraction with the back of his hands against the legs of the chair (*Figure 3-38*).

47. Chair Lift

The athlete is seated in a chair. He grasps the seat of the chair and with bent arms endeavors to pull upward with his arms for a maximal contraction of six seconds. He also does one contraction with his arms extended by shrugging or pulling his shoulders upward (*Figure 3-39*).

Figure 3-38   **Figure 3-39**

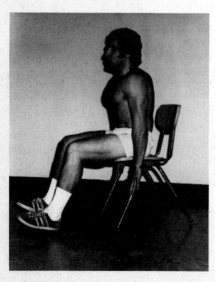

48. Parade Rest Pull

The athlete is standing at parade rest grasping his hands behind his back. He endeavors to pull his arms sideward with his arms extended. He also does one contraction with his elbows flexed (*Figure 3-40*).

49. Overhead Pull

The athlete grasps his hands above his head with his arms extended. He endeavors to pull his extended arms sideward for a maximal contraction of six seconds. He also does one contraction with his elbows flexed (*Figure 3-41*).

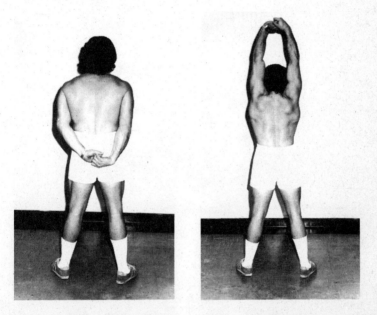

Figure 3-40   **Figure 3-41**

50. Sideward Arm Elevator

The athlete is seated in a chair with his elbows flexed and at his sides. His partner is standing behind him with his hands against the athlete's elbows. The athlete endeavors to lift his elbows against the resistance provided by his partner. He does one contraction of six seconds with elbows at his sides and another with his elbows about eight inches from his body. He also does two contractions with his arms extended—one with his arms at his sides and another with his arms about 45° from his body. His partner grasps his wrists (*Figure 3-42*).

Figure 3-42

51. Sideward Arm Depressor

This exercise is done in the same manner as the "sideward arm elevator" except that the athlete endeavors to depress his arms against the resistance offered by his partner. His partner grasps him on the underside of his elbow or wrist. Four contractions, two with each arm, are done as in the "sideward arm elevator."

52. Forward Extended Arm Elevator

The athlete is standing or seated with his arms extended forward at a 45° angle to his body. His palms are turned downward. His partner holds his wrists down as the athlete endeavors to elevate his extended arms for six seconds against the resistance provided. Another contraction is done with the arms at 90° to the body. Both contractions are repeated with the palms turned upward (*Figure 3-43*).

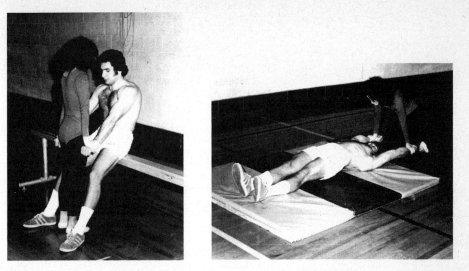

| Figure 3-43 | Figure 3-44 |

53. Pull Over

The athlete is lying on his back on the floor with his arms extended above his head. His partner is holding his wrists. The athlete endeavors to lift his extended arms above his head against the resistance provided by his partner. One contraction of six seconds duration is done with the arms on the floor and another with the arms at a 45° angle to the floor. An additional two contractions are done with the elbows flexed at a 90° angle (*Figure 3-44*).

54. Resisted Push-Up

The athlete endeavors to do a push-up against the resistance provided by his partner. Two six second maximal contractions are made at two different points in the push-up (*Figure 3-45*).

Figure 3-45

EXERCISES FOR THE LEGS AND FEET

55. Sitting Knee Extensor

The athlete is seated on the edge of a chair. He grasps one shin with both hands and endeavors to extend the knee for a maximal contraction of six seconds. He does the same exercise for the opposite leg (*Figure 3-46*).

56. Sitting Leg Adductor

The athlete is seated on the edge of a chair with his knees apart. His arms are crossed with the hands and opposite elbows on the inside of the knees. He endeavors to adduct his legs for a maximal contraction of six seconds (*Figure 3-47*).

57. Sitting Leg Abductor

The athlete is seated on the edge of a chair. His arms are crossed and he is holding the outside of his knees. He endeavors to abduct his legs for a maximal contraction of six seconds (*Figure 3-48*).

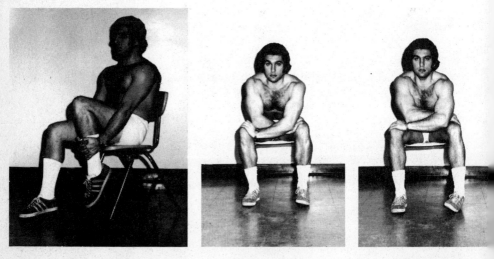

Figure 3-46   Figure 3-47   Figure 3-48

58. Dorsi Flexor on Desk

The athlete is seated in front of a desk. He hooks his feet under the desk and endeavors to dorsiflex his feet (lift his toes with his heels on the floor) against the resistance of the desk for a maximal contraction of six seconds.

59. Foot Abductor

The athlete is seated in a chair with his little toes against the inside of the front legs of the chair. He endeavors to rotate his feet outward against the resistance of the chair legs for a maximal contraction of six seconds or he may do the exercise as it is illustrated (*Figure 3-49*).

60. Foot Adductor

The athlete is seated in a chair with his big toes outside the front legs of the chair. He endeavors to rotate his feet inward against the resistance of the chair legs for a maximal contraction of six seconds or he may do the exercise as illustrated (*Figure 3-50*).

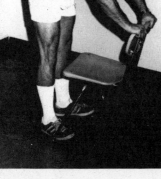
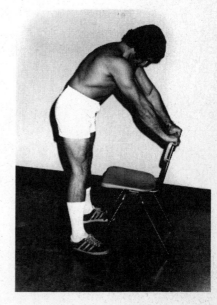

| Figure 3-49 | Figure 3-50 |

61. Rise on Toes in Door Frame

The athlete is standing between the door frame with his arms extended overhead and his hands under the top of the frame. He endeavors to rise on his toes for a maximal contraction of six seconds (*Figure 3-51*).

Figure 3-51

62. Sitting Knee Extensor with Partner

The athlete is sitting on a table or chair. His partner is facing the athlete and holding his knee with one hand and his ankle with the other. The athlete endeavors to extend his knee against the resistance offered by his partner for a maximal contraction of six seconds. Another contraction is also done with the opposite leg (*Figures 3-52 and 3-53*).

Figure 3-52   **Figure 3-53**

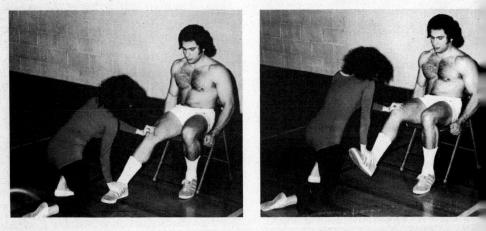

63. Sitting Knee Flexor with Partner

The athlete is sitting on the edge of a table or chair with his knees over the edge of the table. His partner has one hand behind the athlete's upper calf muscle and the other behind his ankle. The athlete endeavors to flex his knee against the resistance offered by his partner for one maximal contraction of six seconds. Another contraction is also done with the opposite leg (*Figure 3-54*).

64. Ankle Eversion and Inversion with Partner

The athlete is sitting on the edge of a table or chair with his knees over the edge. His partner is holding one foot with both hands so that the thumb of one hand is across the top of the foot and the fingers are across the bottom of the foot. The athlete first attempts to evert (turn the inside edge toward the outside) the foot against the resistance offered by his partner for a maximal contraction of six seconds. He then attempts to invert (turn the outside edge toward the inside) the foot against the resistance offered by his partner for a maximal contraction of six seconds (*Figure 3-55*).

Figure 3-54

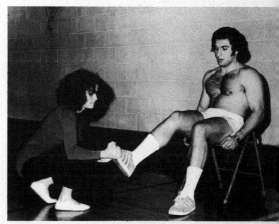
Figure 3-55

EXERCISES FOR THE TRUNK AND NECK

65. Chest Push

The athlete places the palms of his hands against one another in front of his chest. His elbows are flexed and elevated. He endeavors to push his hands against one another for a maximal contraction of six seconds (*Figure 3-56*).

66. Chest Pull

The athlete grasps the wrist of one hand directly in front of his chest or grasps Indian grip as shown. His elbows are flexed and elevated. He endeavors to pull his arms apart while holding his wrist for a maximal contraction of six seconds (*Figure 3-57*).

Figure 3-56   **Figure 3-57**

67. Neck Exercises

The athlete places the palm of one hand against the side of the head and endeavors to push his head sideward against the resistance of his hand. He does one contraction to the other side using the opposite hand. He clasps his hands behind his head and endeavors to push his head backward. He places both palms on his forehead and endeavors to push his head forward.

He places his left hand to the right side of his forehead and endeavors to turn his head to the right. He places his right hand to the left side of his forehead and endeavors to turn his head to the left. He does all six contractions for six seconds each.

68. Seated Dead Lift

The athlete sits deeply into a chair, leans forward slightly and grasps the underside of the seat on each side. He endeavors to bring his back to the vertical position in a maximal contraction of six seconds duration by pulling on the bottom of the chair seat with his arms extended (*Figure 3-58*).

Figure 3-58

69. Seated Shoulder Shrug

The athlete is seated in a chair. He grasps the underside of the chair seat directly under his buttocks in such a manner that his arms are extended and his shoulders are lowered. He endeavors to elevate his shoulders for a maximal contraction of six seconds.

70. Sit-Up with a Partner

The athlete is lying supine on the floor. His partner is kneeling alongside with one hand on the athlete's chest and the other on his knee. She allows the athlete to sit up until his back is at a 45 degree angle to the floor, gradually increasing resistance until she prohibits completion of the sit-up. The athlete endeavors to complete the sit-up against the resistance for a maximal contraction of six seconds (*Figure 3-59*).

Figure 3-59   **Figure 3-60**

71. Prone Back Arch with a Partner

The athlete is lying prone on the floor. His partner is kneeling alongside him with one hand on his upper back and the other on his lower thigh. The athlete endeavors to pull his trunk and thighs off the floor to arch his back against the resistance provided by his partner. A maximal contraction is done for six seconds (*Figure 3-60*).

72. Prone Leg Curl with a Partner

Lying prone on the floor, the athlete flexes the knees until the shins are at a 45° angle to the floor. The partner, who is kneeling on the floor, grasps the ankles. The athlete endeavors to flex the knees in a maximal contraction of six seconds duration against the resistance provided by his partner (*Figures 3-61 and 3-62*).

Figure 3-61   **Figure 3-62**

73. Lying Resisted Side Leg Raiser

The athlete is lying on his side. His partner is kneeling alongside him with one hand on the upper side of his leg and the other against his hip. The athlete endeavors to raise the extended upper leg against the resistance offered by his partner for a maximal contraction of six seconds duration. He rolls to his other side and repeats the exercise with the other leg.

EXERCISES FOR THE WRISTS AND HANDS

74. Wrist Front Curl

The athlete is seated in a chair. He places his right forearm along his right thigh so that his hand projects beyond his knee. He grasps his clenched right fist with his left hand. His right wrist is hyperextended. He endeavors to flex his wrist in a maximal contraction of six seconds duration against the resistance offered by his left hand. He does the same exercise for his left wrist (*Figure 3-63*).

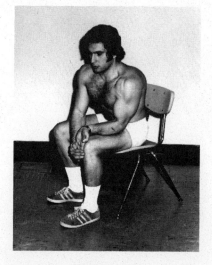

Figure 3-63

75. Wrist Reverse Curl

This exercise is done in the same manner as the wrist front curl except that the palm is turned downward, the wrist is flexed and the athlete endeavors to hyperextend the wrist. One contraction of six seconds duration is done for each wrist.

76. Wrist Pronator and Supinator

The athlete is seated with his right forearm across his upper thigh. He grasps his clenched right fist with his left hand and endeavors to pronate and then to supinate his right hand against the resistance offered by his left hand. He does the same two contractions with his left hand. All four contractions are done for six seconds.

77. Fist Clenching

Simply clenching the fists with maximal contractions is an excellent exercise for increasing the strength of the forearms. A solid rubber ball may be used.

78. Seated Finger Flexor and Extensor Against a Desk

The athlete is seated in front of a desk or table. He places the backs of his wrists against his thighs with his finger tips against the underside of the desk. He endeavors to flex his fingers against the resistance of the desk for a maximal contraction of six seconds duration. He repeats the exercise with the front of his wrists against his thighs endeavoring to hyperextend his fingers for a maximal contraction of six seconds duration.

4

PROCEDURES FOR DEVELOPING ATHLETIC ENDURANCE

Just as different sports place varying muscular demands upon different muscle groups, so do different sports demand different degrees and kinds of endurance. In some sports skills (the press in Olympic lifting, the supine press in power lifting, the crucifix or front lever in gymnastics or some pinning combinations in wrestling) a slow all-out muscular effort is required to overcome a maximal resistance. Other sports skills require power (strength plus speed) in an explosive, quick movement as in the shot put, javelin throw, discus throw, pole vault, broad jump, or high jump in track and field; the vaulting and tumbling events and other specific moves in the other gymnastic events; the kick, pass, and both offensive and defensive linemen's moves in football; batting and throwing in baseball; the start in swimming; the lay-up in basketball; take-downs in wrestling; and the serve or smash in tennis. Other sports skills require a sustained effort repeated many times against a moderate resistance as in swimming, boxing, middle distance running, crew, canoeing, or routines in gymnastics. Still other sports skills require moderate contractions of large muscle groups against little resistance for relatively long periods of time as in distance or cross country running, distance swims, cycling, back packing, skating, cross country skiing, soccer, lacrosse, basketball, handball, tennis, squash, or mountain climbing.

CONDITIONING PROGRAMS FOR DIFFERENT SPORTS

Each sport requires a different kind of endurance. Some place a greater premium upon raw strength, others upon power, and others upon endurance. Consequently, the conditioning program for each must be specially designed. Within a sport, the conditioning program must further be individually designed. Increases in strength will produce increases in muscular endurance as well as increases in power. However, strength and power, and endurance are not the same, are not improved through the same procedures, and are not the result of changes in the same physiologic processes. Each sport requires a specific training program that gives the proper distribution of time to the development of each of the qualities needed and in their relative importance. Obviously, a distance runner should not spend much time in developing the strength and bulk of his arms and upper body. However, it may not be so obvious that in training for power events such as the shot put or snatch in weight lifting, it is inadvisable to use maximum resistances. The reason for this is that it is impossible for the muscles to move with speed in lifting a maximal weight. For this reason, the athlete should periodically use about 75 per cent of his maximal load and do a greater number of repetitions—4 or 5 sets of 4 to 6 repetitions.

DIFFERENCES IN WEIGHT TRAINING PROGRAMS

In those activities in which strength and power are of relatively less importance and endurance is of greater importance, that is, where the body or its parts encounter less resistance but the movement is repeated many times as in canoeing, swimming, or tennis, the weight training program should call for a lighter load but a greater number of repetitions. Here the bar should be loaded to about 50 per cent of maximum and 2 or 3 sets of 15 to 20 repetitions should be done increasing the number of repetitions to 30 to 50 repetitions before increasing the resistance as condition is improved. The use of less resistance and greater repetitions will not call into play or develop muscle fibers in those motor units which require high stimulus for activation, but it will improve the blood supply to the exercised part through improved vascularization.

EFFECTS OF ENDURANCE EXERCISES UPON THE ORGANS

Improved vascularization to exercising muscles is only one aspect, and a minor one at that, of the physiologic modifications which occur as an adaptation to the stress of endurance work. The other changes occur in the cardiovascular, respiratory, parasympathetic, and the digestive systems, in blood, in the bones, and in the function of the glands of internal secretion. These changes are brought about most effectively through activities which are done against little resistance at a pace or speed sufficient to elevate the pulse rate to a minimum of 150 beats per minute and which are sustained for at least 15 minutes. Activities which can meet these criteria include jogging, running, rope skipping, swimming, cycling, circuit training, interval running or swimming, fartlek or speed play, skating, competitive walking, canoeing, cross country skiing and rowing. The activities usually selected to develop circulatory-respiratory endurance are those in which the dosage of activity can be controlled and monitored. For this reason, skating, canoeing, and cross country skiing are not often used in training for cardio/respiratory fitness.

The *Physical Fitness Research Digest* published quarterly by the President's Council on Physical Fitness and Sports has defined circulatory-respiratory endurance as follows: "Circulatory-respiratory endurance is characterized by moderate contractions of large muscle groups for relatively long periods of time, during which maximal adjustments of the circulatory-respiratory system are necessary, as in distance running or swimming." The adjustments which are made enable the body to withstand increasingly greater endurance stresses.

EFFECTS UPON THE HEART

The heart, whose only function is to pump the blood to the body cells, is modified in several ways. The muscular walls or myocardium of the heart become stronger enabling it to eject a greater volume of blood at each systole (contraction) so that both at rest and during a specific amount of work it need not beat as frequently. This means that the heart secures a longer rest period during its relaxation phase (diastole). A longer diastole also permits more time for filling of the atria which results in more blood being ejected during systole. Additionally, the blood supply to the heart is improved through the development of additional and new blood vessels. The coronary network of blood vessels is increased and the heart receives more nutrients and oxygen so that it does not fatigue as quickly.

EFFECTS UPON THE VASCULAR SYSTEM

The vascular system, too, is modified in such manners as to enable it to transport greater amounts of blood. The diameter of arteries and veins increases and the number of arterioles and capillaries increases to facilitate faster transport of blood and consequently faster exchange of oxygen and nutrients into the cells and carbon dioxide and other waste products of combustion out of the cells. This enhances endurance by delaying fatigue caused by the accumulation of lactic acids and oxygen deprivation.

EFFECTS UPON THE BLOOD

The oxygen-carrying capacity of the blood is increased because the number of red blood cells or erythrocytes and the amount of hemoglobin are increased. During strenuous exercise more red blood cells are found per liter in the blood of well conditioned endurance athletes even though their red cell count may be no higher at rest than that of people leading a sedentary life. Additionally, participation in endurance activities produces an increase in the amount of blood. Both of these phenomena delay the onset of physiologic fatigue and enable the heart to meet the demands of the cells with fewer beats.

EFFECTS UPON THE RESPIRATORY SYSTEM

Changes are made in the respiratory system as an adaptation to the stress of endurance work. All these changes enhance tolerance to the stress of endurance work, delay the onset of physiologic fatigue, and enable the athlete to perform at higher levels of skill before suffering the decrements in skill due to fatigue. The respiratory muscles increase in strength permitting greater expansion of the thorax and fuller excursions of the diaphragm. This enables inhalation of a greater volume of air. Fuller respiratory movements facilitate greater venous return. As a result of the diaphragm moving further downward, greater pressure is exerted upon the veins in the abdomen. This pressure compresses the veins in the abdomen and since the veins have valves which permit blood to flow only toward the heart, the pressure pushes the blood in the abdominal veins upward into the thorax. Then as the chest wall collapses during expiration, pressure upon the veins in the thorax is increased and the blood is pushed from the thoracic veins into the venae cavae and into the right atrium. It should not be concluded from the preceding comments that endurance can be improved through deep breathing exercises. These exercises are a total waste of valuable time since the only way in which endurance and even that part of it called maximum oxygen uptake or utlization of oxygen can be increased is through creation of a demand for oxygen at the cellular level. This means there is no magic shortcut. Cardiac and respiratory stress must be undergone through physical activity sufficient to raise the pulse rate to 150 beats per minute or more and this must be sustained for at least 15-30 minutes. Yet, some coaches still have their athletes inhale deeply as they raise their arms high overhead, rise to tip toes, and then bend forward and smash their arms against their abdomen or beat their chest with flailing arms like a bunch of apes! Endurance exercises will increase the number and size of the alveoli and increase the capillary bed around the aveoli and the alveolar ducts which will facilitate gaseous exchange between the blood and the lungs. Faster processing of the blood will contribute toward supplying of greater amounts of oxygen to the muscle cells.

Research has also shown that training enables not only the skeletal muscles involved in a specific physical activity to work with greater efficiency and consequent decreased demand for oxygen but the same happens to the respiratory muscles (diaphragm, intercostals, pectorals, and abdominals). It has also been shown that those who do endurance work learn to tolerate accumulation of greater amounts of lactate in the blood. Lactate accumulates when oxygen intake and delivery is inadequate to meet the demands of the muscle cells for oxygen. This is called anaerobic activity and occurs when an oxygen debt is created as in sprints and runs up to the 440. In aerobic work the intake of oxygen is adequate to meet the demands of muscle cells for oxygen. The most effective endurance work is when the activity is just strenuous enough that maximum oxygen uptake just meets the demands of the cells for oxygen. This is known as the steady state.

CARDIOVASCULAR/RESPIRATORY ENDURANCE PROGRAMS

The coach can select from a number of cardiovascular-respiratory endurance programs. Whatever program he selects, it is advisable that the following principles be observed:

1. Participants should exercise within their tolerance.

2. The dosage should be progressively increased as tolerances are improved.

3. The exercise should be sufficiently intensive to increase the heart or pulse rate to 150 beats per minute or more and the exercise should be sustained at this level for a minimum of 15 minutes. This implies that the exercise program must be individualized since the physical conditions of athletes can vary considerably. Athletes can be taught to take their own pulse. The pulse count is secured by placing the index and two middle fingers against the wrist on the thumb side alongside the tendons about an inch above the heel of the left hand. The count should be taken for 30 seconds and multiplied by 2.

4. Allow 10-15 weeks to achieve results. The conditioning program should be initiated 10-15 weeks before the beginning of the competitive season. This means, for football, starting in June. Many sports are not strenuous enough to sustain optimal physical fitness throughout the season. It has been noted that the physical fitness level is often lower at the end of the season than it was at the beginning of the season. Consequently, it is necessary to continue some fitness work throughout the season. This work should be done after work on skills, techniques, strategy, and teamwork has been completed in order that fatigue will not interfere with skill acquisition. Two sessions per week will be adequate to sustain the fitness level achieved before initiation of the competitive season.

5. When the conditioning program is begun, exercises should be done three days per week for two weeks and then five days per week until regular work on the sports skills and team work is begun.

6. The coach can devise skill drills which can be sustained so that skill and endurance are enhanced simultaneously. The skills must be those in which there is no hazard since timing and coordination are detrimentally affected by fatigue. These drills should be done at the end of the workout. They should not be used for newly learned skills.

CIRCUIT TRAINING

Circuit training consists of seven to twelve stations. A particular exercise is done at each station for a specified number of times. Activities at the several stations can be selected to develop strength, power, or muscular endurance of different muscle groups, to develop agility, or to develop cardiovascular-respiratory endurance. The principle of progressive overload can be put into effect by increasing the number of repetitions or the resistance at each station, and doing the circuit in the same time (develops more endurance), by doing the circuit in less time (develops more speed), by endeavoring to complete as many circuits in a set time as possible (develops more speed or endurance depending on time set), or by endeavoring to complete the circuit in as little time as possible (develops more speed).

The circuit can be adapted to differing conditioning objectives and needs, facilities, equipment and space available, and individual needs. The athletic coach can set up a circuit, instruct athletes in the procedures, and then have them run the circuit at times other than scheduled practice times. Athletes can keep a daily record of their improvement. The severity of the training dose must be sufficiently challenging to insure that a maximal effort is required to complete the circuit. In resistance exercises such as with weights, bar dips and pull-ups, the goal should be approximately half the number of repetitions the performer can do in a 30 second test. In endurance exercises such as the bench step, squat thrust, and running in place, the goal should be half the number of repetitions the performer can do in one minute. These individual goals should be established via testing at the introduction of the program. A one minute rest should be given between tests when establishing the goals for each student.

The stations should be set up so that the circuit finishes near where it began. There should be adequate space between stations so that it will be unlikely that participants will collide with one another in moving from station to station.

A 12-station circuit will accommodate 48 participants (4 beginning at each station) performing simultaneously and continuously. Each station should be numbered with stick figure illustrations and terse printed explanations of the exercise procedure on a cardboard placard attached to the wall.

On the signal, each athlete begins the exercise for his station. He

keeps count of his own repetitions. When he has completed the prescribed number of repetitions, he moves quickly to the next station to
do the prescribed number of repetitions of the exercise for that station.
He proceeds in this manner until he has completed three full circuits or
the number of circuits prescribed by the coach. He must complete the
full number of repetitions at each station before proceeding to the next
station even if he requires a rest between repetitions. Time is recorded
at the completion of the prescribed circuits. A realistic but challenging
"target time" should be established. When this "target time" has
been achieved a new one should be established.

Following are some exercises for use at the different stations:

Squat Thrusts (*Figures 4-1, 4-2, 4-3*):
   (*30-100 times*)

Start	2	3	4	Finish
(At Attention)	Squat Knees Outside Arms	Front Leaning Rest—Trunk And Legs Fully Extended	Squat Position	(Starting Position)

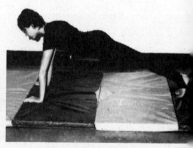

Figure 4-1   **Figure 4-2**   **Figure 4-3**

Push-Ups (*Figures 4-4, 4-5*):

Start	2	Finish
(50% maximum)		(Starting Position)

Keep back straight (no jacknifing or arching), touch chest to floor, return to fully extended position of the arms.

Figure 4-4	Figure 4-5

Ten V-Sits (*Figures 4-6, 4-7*):

Start		Finish
(Supine) (50% maximum)	Touch Toes with hands, legs fully extended	(Starting) Position)

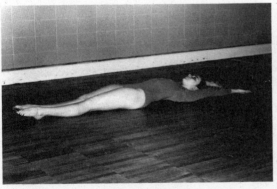

Figure 4-6	Figure 4-7

Back Extensions (*Figure 4-8*):

(50% maximum)

Start (Prone)	2	Finish
Hands clasped behind neck and heels hooked under equipment or hips held down	Pull chest off floor, arch back, head up.	Starting position

Figure 4-8

Running in Place (*Figure 4-9*):

(100 steps)

Knee to chest at each step.

Figure 4-9

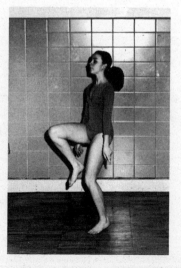

Abdominal Curls:

Start (Prone)	2	Finish
(30-100 times) Hands clasped behind head (*Figure 4-10*).	Curl shoulders off floor	(Return to start) (*Figure 4-11*).

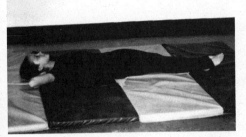

Figure 4-10

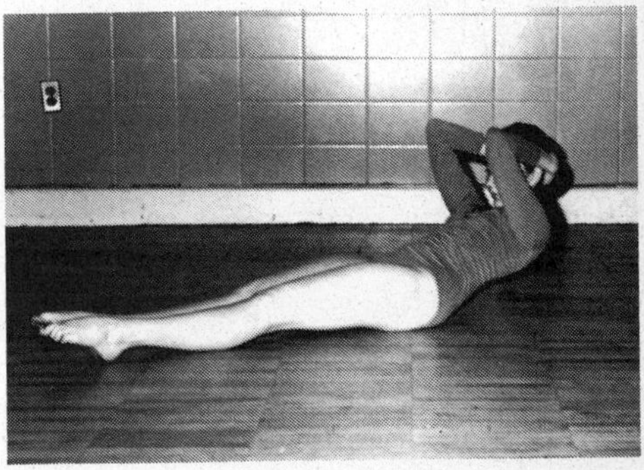

Figure 4-11

Sit-Ups:

	2	3	4	Finish
Start (prone) (30-100 times) Hands clasped behind neck	Touch right elbow to left knee (*Figure 4-12*).	Return to start	Touch left elbow to right knee (*Figure 4-13*).	(Return to start)

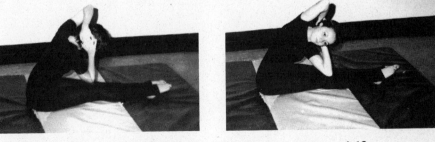

Figure 4-12

Figure 4-13

Bench Step:

(Bench 12-20" high)
(1-2 minutes)

Start	2	3	4	5
Standing in front of the bench both feet on floor	Left foot on bench *(Figure 4-14)*.	Both feet on bench *(Figure 4-15)*.	Left foot on floor *(Figure 4-16)*.	Both feet on floor

Figure 4-14   Figure 4-15   Figure 4-16

Side Straddle Hops:
(30-100 times)

Start	2	Finish
(At Attention)	Feet Apart and Arms Raised Overhead *(Figure 4-17)*	(Start Position)

Lateral Run:

Athletes run sideways to touch first one side line of the freethrow line and then the other. Lines can be extended through use of floor tape to lengthen the course or 10-20 touchings of the side lines of the freethrow lane could be required *(Figure 4-18)*.

Figure 4-17

BASKETBALL END LINE

START

FREE
THROW
LANE

FINISH

Figure 4-18

Pull-Ups (*Figure 4-19*):

(Palms toward athlete) or chin-up (Palms turned away from the athlete (50% of maximum)

Pull chin above bar and then lower to fully extended position of the arms.

Figure 4-19

Trunk Twister:

Start	1	2	3	4
(Figure 4-20)	Touch right hand to left toe (30-100 times) *(Figure 4-21)*	Return to starting position	Touch left hand to right toe	Return to starting position

Figure 4-20   **Figure 4-21**   **Figure 4-22**

Dips:

(Both ends of bars may be used by each of two athletes

	Start		
	(Arms fully extended)	Flex arms until arms are at right angles *(Figure 4-22)*	Push back up to fully extended position of the arms

Press with barbell:

Start	Press	Finish
Bar across chest (50-80% maximum)— 10 repetitions	Arms fully extended upward	Bar across chest

Curl with barbell:

Arms extended (50-80% maximum)— 10 repetitions	Elbows fully flexed—elbows alongside hips	Arms extended

Half squat with barbell:

Start	1	Finish
Bar (3/4 body weight) Across shoulders, behind neck. Towel between bar and neck (50-80% maximum)— 10 repetitions	Flex knees to 55° angle. Keep back as nearly vertical as possible	Use spotter on each end to catch bar

Upright rowing:

Start	1	Finish
Arms extended downward holding bar (50% of maximum)— 10 repetitions	Pull bar up along body to chest. Elbows high and outward	

Sprinter:

Start	1
Front leaning rest with one foot up between hands and other foot as in sprint start, *30-100 times (Figure 4-23)*	Reverse leg positions

The preceding are only a few of the exercises which could be used at the different stations. Some of the others which could be used are:

Prone flutter kicks—25-50 times (*Figure 4-24*)
Rope skipping—2-4 minutes

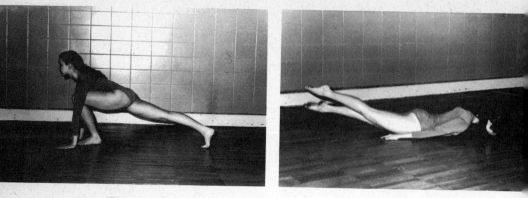

Figure 4-23   **Figure 4-24**

Side benders—30-100 times

Static stretching exercises such as splits, backbends, quadriceps, stretcher, etc.

Use of horizontal ladders (hang-walk across, leg raises, chin-ups, etc.)

Use of vertical ladders (leg raises, back arches, etc.)

Use of bleachers (run up and down).

Use of climbing ropes, balance beams, rowing machines and wall pulleys (*Figures 4-25, 4-26*)

Figure 4-25   **Figure 4-26**

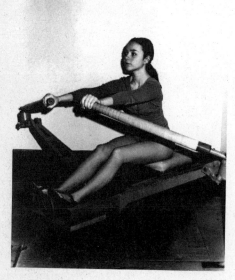

The exercise at each successive station should call into play muscle groups different from those used at the previous station. For example, an abdominal exercise such as the sit-up should follow push-ups. Static stretching exercises should follow endurance events such as running in place or bench steps.

INTERVAL TRAINING

Interval training is a form of progressive conditioning in which the intensity of the activity, the duration of each bout, the number of bouts, the time or kind of rest periods between bouts, or the order of the bouts is varied. Interval training procedures can be applied to cycling, swimming, bench stepping, rope skipping, or running in place as well as forward running. The major objective of the program is to improve endurance by increasing the intensity or duration of bouts, or both, while decreasing time for rest. The program is, for most, less monotonous than continuous endurance work.

First, a realistic goal is established, say to run the mile in 5 minutes. Then this distance is broken down into smaller units and times are decided upon for running these distances and for the length of rest periods between the running of each distance. The athlete could run 110 yards 16 times at a speed of 17 seconds for each run with a two minute rest between each run, endeavoring to decrease the time for each 110 yard run as his endurance improves. When he can do each run at 14 seconds, he reduces the rest period to one and a half minutes and then to one minute. Then he increases the distance of the run to 220 yards at 35 seconds for each of 8 runs with a 3 minute rest between each run. When he can do each 220 yard run in 30 seconds, the rest period is reduced to two and a half minutes, then two minutes, then one and a half minutes, and finally one minute. When this has been accomplished, he does four 440 yard runs at 75 seconds with a three minute rest between each run. After he has reduced this time for each run to 63 seconds, he progressively reduces the rest period to one minute between each run. Then he runs 880 yards twice at 2:30.0 or 150 seconds for each run with a three minute rest between the two runs. When he has reduced his time to 140 seconds or 2:20 he progressively reduces the rest period between runs to one minute. When this has been accomplished he should be able to run the mile in 5 minutes.

The concept of alternately increasing the intensity of the exercise and the distance and decreasing the resting time can be applied to swimming. Athletes swim a set distance (25 yards) several times at progressively faster speeds and then decrease the resting time between swims as condition is improved and then increase the distances in the same manner as in the illustration for the mile run.

When the interval principle is applied to rope skipping the skipping time is progressively increased while the rest period between bouts of skipping is decreased. For example, the athlete could start with 5 one-minute bouts with a one-minute rest between each, then reduce the rest period to one-half minute, then increase the bouts to one and a half minutes with a one minute rest between bouts, then reduce the rest period to one-half minute, then increase the time of each bout to 2 minutes with a one-minute rest, then reduce the rest period to one-half minute. He could proceed in this manner to achieve a goal of five bouts of three minutes each with a half-minute rest between each. He could also increase the number of bouts or the total skipping time.

COOPER'S AEROBICS

Kenneth M. Cooper, M. D. and Major, U.S.A.F. Medical Corps (Retired), who wrote the well known book *Aerobics*[1] has probably done more than anyone else to popularize jogging and other forms of endurance exercises. While his research on thousands of U.S. Army Air Force men and the exercise program he devised based on his findings are directed primarily at laymen rather than athletes, they can be utilized by athletes and their coaches—particularly those involved in endurance events.

As the title of his book indicates, it is not concerned with development of strength, power, flexibility, agility or speed—all qualities needed for success in athletics. It is not concerned with development of anaerobic power which is essential to success in sprint swimming or running, in gymnastics and in many team sports. It is concerned with aerobic power which is necessary in endurance events. Aerobic power is the ability of the body to utilize oxygen and is accepted as the best measure of cardiovascular condition.

Cooper found that the distance covered by running (and walking if necessary) in 12 minutes correlates highly with the milliliters of oxygen the person can process per minute. It is an expensive and time

---

[1]Kenneth H. Cooper, M.D., M.P.H., Copyright © 1968 by Kenneth H. Cooper and Kevin Brown. Reprinted by permission of the publisher, M. Evans and Co., Inc., New York.

consuming process requiring treadmills, gas analysis machines, electrocardiograms and other equipment to measure oxygen consumed per minute. His simple test, though designed for non-athletes, can provide a challenge for athletes. The procedure is simply to see how much distance can be covered in 12 minutes over flat terrain or an indoor or outdoor track. It is well to mark off the track in tenths of miles. The subject may run, jog, or walk. If he becomes breathless, he may walk until he regains his breath. Amount of oxygen consumed and the Physical Fitness Category is based on the distance covered according to the following chart:

Fitness Category	Distance Covered	Oxygen Consumption
I. Very Poor	Less than 1.0 mile	28.0 ml's or less
II. Poor	1.0 to 1.24 miles	28.1 to 34 ml's
III. Fair	1.25 to 1.49 miles	34.1 to 42 ml's
IV. Good	1.50 to 1.74 miles	42.1 to 52 ml's
V. Excellent	1.75 miles or more	52.1 ml's or more

The standards are about one-tenth of a mile lower for men over 35 years of age and two-tenths of a mile lower for women. Cooper estimates that about 80 per cent of the American population falls into the first three categories. The test can also be used as a measure of improvement made during a conditioning program.

Any high school or college athlete who cannot qualify for fitness category IV or V should secure a copy of Cooper's *Aerobics* and begin immediately to improve his cardiovascular condition. The system begins with the above classification test. The subject then progresses within his category until he can earn 30 points each week at which time he moves into the next category. The oxygen cost for specified dosages of exercise in a number of activities such as running, swimming, cycling, walking, stationary running, handball, squash, and basketball has been computed.

To earn 30 points per week, the subject in categories IV or V should run a mile in less than 8 minutes 6 times each week, or a mile in less than 6:30 five times each week, or a mile and a half in less than 12 minutes 4 times each week or 2 miles in less than 16 minutes 3 times each week. Similar standards have been established for the other activities.

The most important feature of the program is the point system which provides a prescription for the amount of exercise, a record of progress, a built-in motivation and progressively increased dosages of exercise. For example, the dosages for running for category III progresses from 1 mile in 12:45 five times per week for 10 points during the first week to 1.5 miles in 11:55 plus 2 miles in 17 minutes twice per week for 31 points during the tenth week.

GRASS DRILLS

Grass drills are useful primarily for development of anaerobic power required for success in activities which use oxygen at a more rapid rate than it can be supplied to the muscle cells. These are activities which have a duration of 30 seconds to 2 minutes such as the 50, 100, 200, or 220 yard swims or runs, gymnastic events, downhill skiing, baseball, speed skating, or weight lifting. Grass drills can also be done in several bouts with a rest period between each bout and thereby develop the specific kind of endurance required for such sports as football, basketball, or soccer in which there are bursts of intense activity interspersed with periods of decreased intensity of activity.

Grass drills should be done in a group. The most efficient method is with the leader in the center of the circle of athletes. The athletes should be spaced at a double arm interval and facing the center. With large groups, two or more concentric circles could be utilized.

On the leader's verbal and performance signal, the athletes begin jogging in place to warm up for 30-60 seconds. Then they run in place lifting the knees up progressively higher until they bounce off the chest. On the signal they drop to a prone or supine position or to a prone position with both legs to the right or left of the long axis of the body. The signals are: "Front!," "Back!," "Right!," "Left!," and "Up!" and are given in random order, the tempo accelerating to a peak and then slowing down finishing in a slow stationary jog for the "warm-down."

The intensity and the duration of the exercises during a bout as well as the length of the rest period (or the tempo of the jogging in place between bouts if this pattern is elected) can be adjusted to conform to the typical patterns of activity of the sport for which the athletes are being conditioned. For example, in basketball and soccer, between bursts of intensive activity, players continue to move about. In doing grass drills to condition for basketball and soccer, the athletes should jog in place between bouts. Gymnasts in competition do routines of 30-60 seconds duration in an event and secure about a 3-5 minute rest before being called up to present a routine in another event. Grass drills for gymnasts should consist of 6 one-minute bouts with a rest of 2-3 minutes between each bout. In football, a play lasts 3-10 seconds with no activity for 10-15 seconds until the next play begins. Grass drills for football players should consist of approximately 20 10-second bouts with a rest of 10 seconds between each bout.

Experimentation with the intensity and length of bouts, length of the rest periods between bouts and the number of bouts is advisable for a particular team since the average fitness level of different teams varies somewhat. The principle of progression should, of course, be utilized by progressively increasing the intensity of each bout and the length of each bout, decreasing the length of the rest period between bouts and increasing the number of bouts. See High knee lift (*Figure 4-53*) and *Figure 4-54*.

WIND SPRINTS

Wind sprints have been used for many years by coaches and physical training personnel in the armed services. In view of the heavy loads done in conditioning work today, the practice of former years of having athletes do wind sprints once or twice across the length of the field seems a mere token.

In wind sprints, the athletes assume the sprinter's starting position along a line and on the whistle or the signal "Go!" "blast out" and sprint until the next whistle or the signal "Stop!" at which time they stop as quickly as possible and drop into the sprinter's starting position again. This procedure is repeated until the field has been traversed any number of times.

Variations in conditioning effects can be produced by varying the distance run between whistles and by varying the total distance run. However, the principle value in wind sprints is in the development of anaerobic power for bursts of intensive activity of 3-20 seconds duration. Wind sprints have built-in motivation since the athletes usually want to race one another.

CYCLING

Knute Rockne of Notre Dame often used cycling as a change from the routine conditioning work and thereby helped to avoid the onset of staleness in his team members. He would have the entire squad go on a long bike trip. Bud Wilkinson has called cycling a complete exercise which develops the legs, arms, back, and abdomen. Carl Snavely has had his team members utilize cycling in the spring to develop endurance and stamina for the fall competitive season.

Although cycling would not contribute adequately to such fitness qualities as strength, power, agility and flexibility and from an administrative point of view, would likely not be the preferred activity for development of team members' endurance, it can serve as an effective and interesting diversion. Distance covered and speed should be progressively increased. A distance of 4 miles could be covered in 13 minutes 5 days for a week and then done in 12 minutes for 5 days the succeeding week. Then during the third week 5 miles could be done in 16 minutes and decreased to 14 minutes the succeeding week. The program could be continued increasing the distance one week and decreasing the time the succeeding week until the athlete is able to do 10 miles in 30 minutes. This kind of program will develop aerobic power. A cycling program could also be designed to develop anaerobic power. This kind of program would require all-out sprints of 1/4—1/2 mile followed by slow peddling for 1/4—1/2 mile and covering a total distance of 5-15 miles for a total of 5-30 sprints. The distance of both the sprints and the slow peddling should conform as nearly as possible to the intermittant distribution of energy bursts in the sport for which the athlete is being conditioned. Shorter and more frequent sprints would be appropriate for football players. Longer and less frequent sprints would be appropriate for soccer forwards and backs while midfield soccer players, since they participate in both offense and defense and are continuously active, should cycle continuously at relatively high speeds but with periodic bursts of speed.

ROPE SKIPPING

Rope skipping is an excellent activity for developing anaerobic power from several points of view.

1. The dosage of exercise can be controlled from the standpoint of both time and intensity.
2. A considerable work load can be done in a short period of time.
3. It is inexpensive. No. 10 sash cord, which can be purchased at any hardware store, serves best. The ends can be knotted or taped. Ropes should be 11 to 13 feet in length. The equipment manager or a student aide could prepare the ropes.

4. Rope skipping can be done individually or in very large groups of up to 100.
5. It can be done indoors or outdoors.
6. No special facility is required.
7. It is economical in terms of time.
8. It can be made interesting through the introduction of a great variety of skills.
9. It is easily administered. Team members form a circle or two or more concentric circles around the leader. Spacing between individuals should be adequate to allow for freedom of movement in swinging the rope.

Techniques

The rope should be grasped between the thumb and the second joint of the first finger. The rope should be turned by wrist rather than elbow action. The hands, while turning the rope, should describe a circle 6-8 inches in diameter. The upper arms should be held close to the trunk while the forearms are angled outward about 45 degrees from the trunk so that the hands are 8-10 inches from the hips. The body should be erect with the head up, no forward bend at the hips and no rounding of the back. The jump should be just high enough to clear the rope—about one inch—and from the balls of the feet with only slight knee and hip flexion. The major portion of the spring should come from the feet and ankles.

Lead-up Skills

The athletes should first practice jumping correctly without the rope. Hop 100 times about one inch above the floor or ground landing on the balls of the feet with the head up, body erect, only slight flexion at hips and knees and with the arms alongside the body. Next, spin the rope with the right hand only 100 times, both ends of the rope being held in this hand. The upper arm should be close to the chest, and the forearm should be flexed to a 45 degree angle so that the hand is 8-10 inches from the hips and the hand should describe a circle 6-8 inches in diameter. Now do 100 spins with the rope held in the left hand. Finally, do 100 hops while spinning the rope first with the right hand and then 100 hops while *spinning* the rope with the left hand. Repeat these procedures spinning the rope backwards. The athletes are now ready to do the basic rope skip. They should start with the rope on the floor behind their heels and spin it up over their head and down in front to hop over it. Three hundred to five hundred rotations should convince them that rope skipping is a pretty good conditioning activity and can be challenging to athletes as well as to small girls and boxers.

The basic skip can be made more challenging by seeing who can do the most skips in 3, 4, 5, or 6 minutes (if a miss occurs, the skipping is resumed and the count is picked up at the number of the miss), by seeing who can do the most skips before missing, or by seeing who can continue skipping the longest without missing five consecutive times. (Their tongues will hang out!)

Skills and Variations:

1. Hop on the right foot only
2. Hop on the left foot only (*Figure 4-27*)
3. Hop alternately on the right and left foot
4. Run in place (*Figure 4-28*)
5. Run forward (*Figure 4-29*)
6. Run backward (*Figure 4-30*)
7. Hop on one foot while holding the opposite leg extended forward parallel to the floor
8. Straddle the legs sideward between hops (*Figure 4-31*)
9. Straddle the legs forward and backward between hops (Keep the body weight evenly distributed on both feet). (*Figure 4-32*)
10. Alternately cross the right leg in front of the left leg and the left leg in front of the right leg between hops. (*Figure 4-33*)
11. Click the heels together between hops. (*Figure 4-34*)
12. Hop in a full squat position. (Keep the back vertical). (*Figure 4-35*)
13. Do all the preceding stunts while turning the rope backward. (The hands must be slightly behind the hips.)
14. As the rope comes up over the head while turning it forward, cross the arms at the elbows and "flip" the wrists to keep momentum on the end of the rope. Continue turning the rope with the arms crossed.
15. Alternately cross and uncross the arms.

Rope skipping can be done in interval fashion by skipping rapidly for 45 seconds to 2 minutes with rest periods of 30-60 seconds between

Figure 4-27

Figure 4-28

Figure 4-29

Figure 4-30

Figure 4-31

Figure 4-32

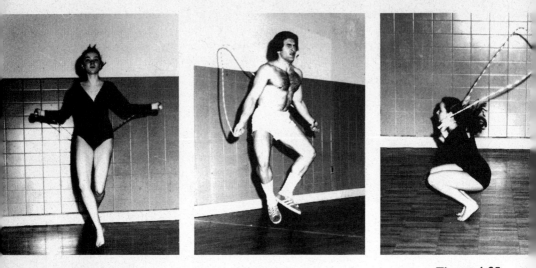

Figure 4-33   **Figure 4-34**   **Figure 4-35**

each of 5-20 bouts. In this form, rope skipping is an excellent activity for developing anaerobic power. To develop aerobic power the skipping should be done at as slow a pace as possible for as long as possible.

CURETON'S PROGRESSIVE, RHYTHMICAL, NONSTOP EXERCISES

Dr. Thomas K. Cureton, Professor Emeritus of the University of Illinois, has developed a conditioning procedure which he has utilized for many years to effect phenomenal improvement in the physical fitness status of adult and middle-aged men. The system includes a series of over 16 lessons progressing from what Cureton calls low to middle to high gear. Each lesson is considerably more intensive and strenuous than the preceding one. Each lesson includes several new exercises. All muscle groups are involved in different ways. While the lessons include exercises which develop flexibility, exercises which develop balance, exercises which develop agility, exercises which develop power and exercises which develop muscular endurance, the primary emphasis is upon development of cardiovascular endurance. Jogging and other forms of endurance work play a prominent role in the lessons. The lessons are designed to develop both aerobic and anaerobic power. Rest periods or slower paced work is interspersed between bouts of intensive effort to incorporate the principles of interval training.

There can be little doubt that both high school and college varsity athletes in most sports would profit from utilization of these procedures. It is certain that they will find the "high gear" sessions sufficiently challenging. Most athletes will probably be unable to complete these high gear lessons until they have improved their endurance. Athletes should not progress to the next lesson until they can complete all of the preceding lessons exactly as prescribed. For fall sport athletes, the conditioning program should begin in June and continue through August—a period of three months. Other athletes should plan to begin their conditioning program three months previous to be beginning of practice sessions in their sport.

A number of sample lessons from Cureton's Progressive, Rhythmical, Nonstop Exercises as adapted by the Cambridge Y.M.C.A. are presented below.

Lesson 3—Low Gear

(30 minutes)

I.   *Talk* on nature of the workout: (a) Need for progressive warm-up, (b) Need to reach all main muscular groups.

II.   *Warm-up Exercises:* (10 minutes total)
1. Walking and jogging around gym.
2. Practice deep breathing and stretching shoulders and chest while walking—jogging—breathing—repeat.
3. Running in place and inhaling deeply.

III.   *Arm, Shoulder and Chest Exercises:* (10 minutes total)
4. Cross-body double arm circles
5. Crawl strokes, forward.
6. Crawl strokes, backward.
7. Arm circle full length (large circles).
8. Arm circle full length (small circles).
9. Push-ups from knees.
10. Extend arms backward repeatedly.
11. Jumping jacks with hands clasped overhead and against thighs.

IV.   *Waist Exercises:* (5 minutes)
12. Cross-over, touch floor and whip back; left then right and repeat. *(Figure 4-36)*

13. Sitting twist to right then to left with arms extended, full length (*Figure 4-37*).
14. Backward extension sitting on heels (*Figure 4-38*).

Figure 4-36   **Figure 4-37**   **Figure 4-38**

V.   *Abdominal, Lower Back and Waist Exercises:* (10 minutes)
   15. Lying on right side, side leg kicks, narrow (*Figure 4-39*).
   16. Lying on left side, side leg kicks, narrow.
   17. Flutter kicks on the front.
   18. Flutter kicks on the back (*Figure 4-40*).
   19. Trunk bending forward (*Figures 4-41, 4-42, 4-43*).
   20. Sitting tucks, hands on hips (*Figure 4-44*).
   21. Chest raising, partner holding hips (*Figure 4-45*).
   22. Sit-ups, hands at sides, or behind neck (*Figure 4-46*).
VI. *Legs and Feet Exercises:* (10 minutes)
   23. Rhythmical alternate leg kicks, forward.
   24. Rhythmical alternate leg kicks, sideward.
   25. Push-ups, leaning against wall.
   26. Hopping around gym on alternate foot (*Figure 4-47*).
   27. Vertical jump (20).
   28. Straddle jump (50).
   29. Scissor jump (50) (*Figures 4-48 and 4-49*).

Figure 4-39

Figure 4-40

Figure 4-41

Figure 4-42

Figure 4-43

Figure 4-44

Figure 4-45

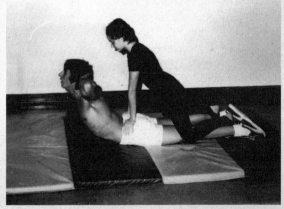

Figure 4-46

Figure 4-47

Figure 4-48   **Figure 4-49**

VII.   *Endurance:*
       30. Run around gym 10 times at moderate speed; last lap
           all-out.
VIII. *Recuperation:* (Train-down routine)
       Walk with relaxing, stretching, breathing exercises.

Lesson 4—Low Gear

I.   *Talk:* Progression in a single workout is to do an exercise for 1 minute, rest—breathe—stretch; then do it again for 2 minutes, followed by rest—breathe—stretch; then do it again for 3 minutes. At the end of the last exercise, the pulse rate and blood pressure will show the stress built up or the adjustment obtained. (5 minutes). Gradual build up will prevent muscle strains.

II. *Walk on Treadmill:* (4 miles/hr., 8.6% grade, long strides) (1 minute).

III. Row on Push-Pull (Row-Tow) machine: (30 strokes/min.) (1 minute)

IV. Step up and down on bench: (14″ high) (30/min. rate) (1 minute)

V.   Repeat II for 2 minutes.

VI. Repeat III for 2 minutes.

VII. Repeat IV for 2 minutes.

VIII. Repeat II for 3 minutes.

IX. Repeat III for 3 minutes.

X.   Repeat IV for 3 minutes.

XI. Pulse rates and blood pressures after workout X.

Lesson 5—Low Gear

I.   *Talk:* Cardiovascular fitness related to energy, metabolism, heart. (10 minutes).

II. *Warm-up Exercises:*

1. Walk a lap, then jog a lap.
2. Walk a lap, then jog 2 laps.
3. Walk a lap, then jog 3 laps.
4. Walk a lap, then jog 4 laps.
5. Walk a lap, then jog 5 laps.

III. *Stretch and Breathe for Recuperation:* (5 minutes)

6. Walk 2 laps, stretch arms, shoulders, chest, waist, knees, ankles—*with deep breathing.*

IV. *Partner Organization:*

7. Line up and count off in "twos."

V.   *Body Exercises:* (15 minutes)

8. Lying on front, chest raisings (15 times), partner holding feet; then change about.

9. Lying on back, sit-ups (15 times), partner holding feet, then change about.
10. Lying on front, leg raisings (15 times) partner holding back, then change about (*Figure 4-50*).
11. Lying on back, double leg raisings (15 times) (*Figure 4-51*).
12. Lying on side, sideward raisings (15 times on each side) partners holding forelegs in arm-lock.

Figure 4-50   **Figure 4-51**

VI.   *Foot and Leg Exercises:* (5 minutes)
13. Walk across gym and back on outside edges of feet.
14. Walk across gym and back with heel-to-toe prance.
15. Hop across gym on right foot only.
16. Hop across gym on left foot only.

VII.   *Postural Exercises:* (5 minutes)
17. Lying on back, take in deep breath and then flatten lower back to floor for 5 seconds; repeat 10 times, exhaling with release.
18. Facing wall, leaning forward, then push up and down on toes.
19. Lying on side, raise top leg up and down in fast side kick: repeat on other side (1 minute each) (*Figure 4-52*).
20. Sitting, hands on floor at hips, sitting tucks (1 minute)

Figure 4-52

VIII. *Hand and Shoulder Exercises:* (10 minutes)
    21. Hang from top stall bar (1 minute)
    22. Stand on lowest stall bar, low grip, swing back and down to hamstring full stretch (keep legs straight).
    23. Put feet up bars, rest on shoulders, grip bars and pull in close, bicycle upside down.
    24. Row, push-ups, pull pulleys, throw medicine balls (10 minutes).

IX. *Wind-up:* Run on treadmill (or on floor), then walk down to recovery.

Lesson 6—Low Gear

I. *Talk:* Value of deep breathing with exercises and recuperation.

II. *Warm-up Exercises:* (15 minutes)
    1. Walk a lap, then jog a lap.
    2. Walk a lap, then jog 2 laps.
    3. Walk a lap, then jog 4 laps.
    4. Walk a lap, then jog 6 laps.
    5. Walk a lap, then jog 8 laps.

III. *Breathing and Stretching for Recuperation:* (5 minutes)
    6. Walk 2 laps: stretch arms, shoulders, chest, waist, knees, and ankles.

IV.   *Organization for Partner Work:* (5 minutes)
    7. Line up and count off in "twos."
    8. Stretch each other, "Twos" stretch "Ones."
    9. Stretch each other, "Ones" stretch Twos."

V.   *Breathing and Breath Holding:* (6 minutes)
    10. Run in place 2 minutes, then hold breath 10 seconds.
    11. Lie on back, deep inhalation and flatten back while holding breath; repeat 10 times.
    12. Run in place 2 minutes, then hold breath 15 seconds.
    13. Lie on back, deep inhalation and flatten back (as in #11)

VI.   *Hard Body Exercises:* (10 minutes)
    14. Sitting tucks (1 minute).
    15. Squat jumps (1 minute).
    16. Side leg raisings (1 minute on each side).
    17. Hang on stall bars (1 minute).
    18. Lie on back, feet up stall bars, push up against bars with feet (3 seconds on and 3 seconds off) (15 times).
    19. Row, push-ups, pull pulleys, throw medicine balls (10 minutes).
    20. Wind-up: Run on treadmill (or on floor), then walk down to recovery.

Lesson 7—Low Gear

I.   *Talk:* Value of Hard Exercises (5 minutes)

II.   *Warm-up Exercises:* (15 minutes)
    1. Walk fast 1 lap.
    2. Jog 2 laps.
    3. Walk fast 1 lap.
    4. Jog 3 laps.
    5. Walk fast 1 lap.
    6. Jog 4 laps.
    7. Walk fast 1 lap.
    8. Jog 5 laps.

III.   *Breathing and Stretching for Recuperation:* (5 minutes)
    9. Walk 2 laps; stretch arms, shoulders, chest, waist, knees, and ankles.

IV. *Organization for Partner Work:* (6 minutes)
    10. Line up and count off in "Twos."
    11. Sit facing each other, legs over partner's legs, hold hands, pull and stretch.
    12. Sit facing each other, feet to feet, hold hands, pull and stretch (*Figure 4-53*).
    13. Back to back, lock arms, pull and stretch (*Figures 4-54 and 4-55*).

Figure 4-53

Figure 4-54   **Figure 4-55**

V.   14. Sitting—take two deep breaths, hold third breath for 10 seconds.

15. Jog two laps, sit down, take two deep breaths, hold third breath 15 seconds.

16. Lie on back, deep inhalations and flatten back; then hold breath 20 seconds.

VI.   *Hard Body Exercises:* (30 minutes)

17. Sitting back to back, push and stand up (2 minutes).

18. Line up, throw medicine ball over head, between legs, over head, etc. (3 minutes).

19. In two lines, overhead throw of medicine ball to partner (3 minutes).

20. In two lines, chest pass of medicine ball to partner (3 minutes).

21. In two lines, underhand pass of medicine ball to partner (3 minutes).

22. Flutter kick on front (2 minutes) (*Figure 4-56*).

23. Lying on back, feet up—apart—together—down (2 minutes)

24. Sit-ups (2 minutes).

25. V-sits (1 minute).

26. Flutter kicks on back (2 minutes).

27. Lying on stomach, hold feet, push and pull (2 minutes).

28. Lying on stomach—rock (1 minute).

29. Inverted cycling (2 minutes) (*Figure 4-57*).

30. Sitting—waist torsion, right and left (2 minutes).

Figure 4-57

Figure 4-56

Lesson 10—Circuit Training—Middle Gear

I.   *Talk:* Explanation of circuit training, alternation of running laps around the gym with several types of muscular endurance exercises involving muscles not much used in running.

II.   *Warm-up:*

    1. Run two laps, walk two.

    2. Run four laps, walk two.

    3. Run six laps, walk two.

    4. Run eight laps, walk two.

    5. Run ten laps, walk two.

III.   *Circuit Training:*

    6. *Sitting tucks,* nearly all out.

    7. Run 5 laps and walk one.

    8. *Flutter kicks on front,* nearly all out.

    9. Run 5 laps and walk one.

    10. *Side leg raisings,* nearly all out.

    11. Run 5 laps and walk one.

    12. *Push-ups,* nearly all out.

    13. Run 5 laps and walk one.

    14. *Double leg raisings,* nearly all out.

    15. Run 5 laps.

IV.   *Recuperation:* Walk it off, 8 to 10 laps.

Lesson 11—Middle Gear

Alternate Leg Work and Arm Work

I.   *Talk:* Mid-course check on brachial pulse wave, blood pressure and pulse rate. (Done in Human Performance Lab—if you have one.)

II.   *Leg Work:* Step 3 minutes on bench, walk 1, jog 1.

III.   *Arm Work:* Pulleys, row, or medicine ball heaves (5 minutes).

IV.   *Leg Work:* Run 3 minutes on treadmill, walk 1, jog 2 (or step 3 minutes on bench).

V.   *Arm Work:* Repeat III for 5 minutes.

VI.   *Leg Work:* Step 4 minutes on bench (or treadmill run), walk 2, jog 3.

VII.   *Arm Work:* Repeat III for 5 minutes.

VIII. *Leg Work:* Step 5 minutes on bench (or treadmill run). Walk 2, jog 3.

IX.   *Repeat heartograph* for fatigue decrement.

X.   *Recuperation:* Walk it off.

Lesson 12—Middle Gear

(60 minutes)

I.   *Talk:* Remind the people of the importance of doing the exercises at home.

II.   *Warm-up:* Run 2 laps, walk 1; run 4 laps, walk 1; run 6 laps, walk 1; run 8 laps, walk 1; run 10 laps.

III.   *Free Exercises:*

A) *Arms and Shoulders:*
1. Standing—front crawl (2 minutes)
2. Standing—back crawl (2 minutes)
3. Loose arm swing (2 minutes)

B) *Trunk:*
4. Sitting—arms horizontal—swing side to side (3 minutes).
5. Sit-ups (1 minute)
6. Sitting tucks (1 minute)
7. Lying on back—feet up—apart—together—down (2 minutes)
8. Standing—trunk rotation—side to side (2 minutes) (*Figures 4-58 and 4-59*).

IV.   *Individual Circuit Training:*

Station 1—side leg raise (Right side) (Left side) 10, 15, 20, 25.

Station 2—Push-ups, 10, 15, 20, 25.

Station 3—Sitting tucks, 10, 15, 20, 25.

Station 4—Vertical jump, 10, 15, 20, 25.

Start at Station 1, do exercise 10 times, run one complete lap to station 2, do exercise 10 times, etc. On second round do exercises 15 times; on third round do exercises 20 times; on fourth round do exercises 25 times.

Figure 4-58   **Figure 4-59**

V.   *Repeat Free Exercises:*
    A) Arms and shoulders
    B) Trunk
VI. *Repeat Individual Circuit Training*
VII. *Recovery:* Walk around gym (5 minutes)

Lesson 13—Middle Gear

(60 Minutes)

I.   *Talk:* Explanation of the exercise routine.
II. *Warm-up:* Run 2 laps, walk 1; run 4 laps, walk 1; run 6 laps, walk 1; run 8 laps, walk 1; run 10 laps.
III. *Team Competition:* (Divide squad into 2 equal teams)
    1. Running relays: (2 laps around gym for each individual)
    2. Jumping relays: (Hopping 1 length of the gym)
    3. Walking relays: (Walking at top speed 2 laps around gym)

IV. *Individual Circuit Training:*
   Station 1: V-sit—30-40-50-60 seconds
   Station 2: Flutter kicks on back—100-150-200-250
   Station 3: Flutter kicks on front—100-150-200-250
   Station 4: Stick body—30-40-50-60 seconds (*Figure 4-60*)
   Run one complete lap around gym between each station.
V. *Taper off and Recovery:*
   1. Jog 5 times around gym.
   2. Walk 5 times around gym.

Figure 4-60

Lesson 15—High Gear

(60 minutes)

Endurance Work

I. *Talk:* Explanation of the high gear exercise. Routine of the lesson. (1) the voluntary psychological limits, (2) use one muscle group all-out only once, (3) some best between bouts, while moving and deep breathing.

II. *Warm-up:* Run 2 laps, walk 1; run 4 laps, walk 1; run 6 laps, walk 1; run 8 laps, walk 1; run 10 laps; walk 3 minutes.

III. *All-out Exercises:*
   1. Chinning—"all-out"—record number done.

    2. Walk around gym once, slowly, breathe deeply.

    3. Vertical jump—"all-out"—record number done.

    4. Walk around gym once, slowly, breathe deeply.

    5. Sit-ups—"all-out"—record number done.

    6. Walk around gym once, slowly, breathe deeply.

    7. Stick-body—"all-out"—record number done.

    8. Walk around gym once, slowly, breathe deeply.

    9. Burpee, or squat thrust—"all-out"—record number done. (*Figures 4-1, 4-2, 4-3*)

    10. Walk around gym once, slowly, breathe deeply.

    11. Push-ups—"all-out"—record number done.

    12. Walk around gym once, slowly, breathe deeply.

IV.   *Relaxation:* Jog around gym twice; walk around gym once.

V.   *Repetition of Exercises*

VI.   *Taper off and Recovery:*

    1. Jog 5 laps around gym, slowly.

    2. Walk 5 laps around gym, breathe deeply and stretch.

    3. Jog 1 lap around gym.

    4. Walk, breathe deeply and stretch until recovered. Put legs up wall and do "bicycle."

    5. Massage calves, thighs, and take a *hot* then *cold* shower.

Lesson 16—High Gear

(60 minutes)

Endurance Work

I.   *Talk:* (1) Announcement of testing sessions. (2) Explanation of lesson procedures.

II.   *Warm-up:* Run 2 laps, walk 1; run 4 laps, walk 1; run 6 laps, walk 1; run 8 laps, walk 1; run 10 laps, walk 3 laps.

III.   *All-out Exercises:*

    1. V-sit for time—"all-out"—record number done.

2. Walk around gym once, slowly, breathe deeply.
3. Side leg raising (right side)—"all-out"—record number done.
4. Walk around gym once, slowly, breathe deeply.
5. Side leg raising (left side)—"all-out"—record number done.
6. Walk around gym once, slowly, breathe deeply.
7. Trunk extension for height—"all-out"—record number done.
8. Walk around gym once, slowly, breathe deeply.
9. Agility exercise—"all-out"—record number done.
10. Walk around gym once, slowly, breathe deeply.
11. Jack springing continuously—"all-out"—record number done.
12. Walk around gym once, slowly, breathe deeply.

IV. *Outside Run:* Run down stairs and run two times around outside playing field, run inside and up stairs in gym.

V. *Relaxation:* Jog around gym twice, walk around gym twice.

VI. *Repetition of All-out Exercises*

VII. *Taper off and Recovery:*
1. Jog 5 laps around gym slowly.
2. Walk 5 laps around gym slowly.
3. Jog 1 lap around gym slowly.
4. Walk, breathe deeply and stretch until recovered. Lie on back, breathe deeply and relax.

Ten Endurance Workouts—High Gear

I.   100-mile running club (only whole miles count, qualification after running 100 cumulative miles).

II.   Marathon swim (laps in pool to total 26 miles).

III.   Run a mile—row a mile (or on rowing machine, 10 minutes)—swim a mile, continuously on one day.

IV.   Work out an hour in gym, continuously (showing warm-up, pressurizing and tapering off stages).

V.   Hike 20 miles (continuously on one day).

VI.   In 3 successive weeks:

    1. Run a lap, walk a lap, and repeat 20 times.

    2. Run 2 laps and walk 1; run 4 laps and walk 1; run 6 laps and walk 1; run 8 laps and walk 1; run 10 laps and walk 1.

    3. Run 10 laps and walk 1; run 8 laps faster and walk 1; run 6 laps faster and walk 1; run 4 laps faster and walk 1; sprint 2 laps and walk 10.

VII.   Chin the bar, all-out; push ups, all-out; sitting tucks, all-out; side leg raises, right, all-out; side leg raises, left, all-out; squat jumps, all-out.

VIII.   Walk 30 minutes on treadmill, up 8.6% grade, continuously at 3-1/2 mi./hr.

IX.   Jog 15 minutes on treadmill (up-grade), continuously at 5 mi./hr.

X.   Throw a javelin, boomerang, medicine ball, football or baseball 50 times, then run to recover and bring object back to start each time on the run (in a single workout).

5

PROCEDURES FOR DEVELOPING ATHLETIC AGILITY AND BALANCE

ATHLETIC AGILITY

Agility is generally defined as the ability to change direction quickly and effectively while moving as nearly as possible at full speed. Factor analyses have shown that agility is accounted for by explosive strength or power. It has been pointed out that power is dependent upon strength and speed of contraction of muscle fiber. The speed of contraction of muscle fiber is dependent upon the viscosity of the muscle fibers and the speed of transmission of the nervous impulse. These are inherited or genetic qualities and the athlete can do nothing about them. However, he can increase his strength and consequently his power and thereby improve his ability.

Nature of Agility:

Changing directions repeatedly as in doing burpees or dodging around obstacles (standard tests of agility) involves alternate concentric and eccentric contractions of involved muscle groups. For example, in dodging around chairs (or opponents) the athlete must decelerate as he is about to change direction. To do this his knee and hip extensors undergo eccentric (lengthening) contractions as they slow the forward momentum of the body. Then they must quickly undergo a concentric contraction of the power type as they force the body in the new direction. Agility movements require alternate decreasing and increasing of momentum.

Momentum equals mass times velocity. An individual athlete's mass is relatively constant but his velocity can be increased through practice and through increasing strength. Of two athletes who weigh the same (same mass) the one with the stronger muscles involved in the agility test will score higher. Of two athletes of identical strength of muscles involved in the agility test, the one who weighs least will score highest in the agility test. An athlete can improve his agility test scores by increasing his strength.[1,2]

A few readers may recall the obstacle courses used by the armed services and in some high school and college physical education programs during World War II. These were designed to develop the specific kinds of agility demanded of combat soldiers. There were ditches to jump, pipes to crawl through, barbed wire to wiggle under, logs over ditches to balance-walk across and vertical, angled, or horizontal ropes to traverse hand over hand. These events probably contributed little to the specific kinds of agility needed in basketball, football, soccer, lacrosse, tennis, or handball. In all these sports the agility required is starting, stopping, and changing direction quickly while upright. Players run forward, sideward, change pace and sometimes must change from forward to backward movement. Consequently, agility drills for these athletes must involve running and quick changes of direction.

---

[1]Baley, James A., "Effects of Isometric Exercises Done with a Belt upon the Physical Fitness Status of College Students," *Research Quarterly*, October, 1966.

[2]Baley, James A., "A Comparison of the Effects upon Selected Measures of Physical Fitness of Participation in Sports and in a Program of Mass Isometric Exercises Done with a Belt," *Journal of Sports Medicine and Physical Fitness*, December, 1967.

Agility Exercises

Several of the exercises presented in the chapter on endurance exercises in the section on anaerobic exercises can also be used to improve agility. These include *grass drills* and *wind sprints*. When wind sprints are used to develop agility, in addition to starting and stopping quickly, players can run 45 or 90 degrees right or left or reverse directions and run backward. Signals such as "45 degrees left," "90 degrees right," or "reverse" can be used in addition to "Stop" and "Go."

Another agility exercise is shuffling sideways as quickly as possible between two lines about 8 feet apart. The element of competition can be added by seeing who can touch the sidelines the greatest number of times in ten, twenty, or thirty seconds.

The most effective agility drills for specific sports are those which incorporate the specific skills of the sport. Coaching texts for specific sports describe a number of these and they will not be repeated here. It is important to mention that since agility involves accuracy, speed, and skill and that since these qualities depreciate rapidly with the onset of fatigue, the drills should not be practiced to the point of fatigue. They should be done at the beginning of the conditioning period and the drills should be short, frequent, and distributed throughout the first half of the practice period.

Strength and skill are the most important factors in agility. Strength in the muscles involved in the specific agility movement must be developed. In sports requiring dodging, this would be principally in the extensors of the hips, knees, and ankles. Consequently, half squats, rise on toes, dead lifts, squat jumps, burpees, and rope skipping are recommended. With respect to the development of skill, agility drills should simulate as nearly as possible the actual game situation. As has been mentioned earlier, texts on the coaching of specific sports describe many of these drills. These drills also develop the specific skills of the sport such as dribbling and passing in soccer and basketball, cradling and passing in lacrosse or evading opponents in football. Examples of such drills are: two (or three) on two in lacrosse, soccer or basketball, dribbling in figure eights around obstacles, or dribbling back and forth between two lines against time.

ATHLETIC BALANCE

There are two principle kinds of balance—static balance (in which stationary balance is held) and dynamic balance (in which balance while moving must be maintained). Each kind of balance is specific. Tests of the two types of balance do not correlate highly with one another. Balance can be further classified into the ability to maintain total body balance with the eyes closed (gross body equilibrium) and the ability to maintain balance with the eyes open (balance with visual cues).

Physiology of Balance

Balance depends on nerve impulses originating in the labyrinth of the inner ear, specifically the otolith organs and the semicircular canals. The labyrinthine reactions are of two types—acceleratory reflexes and positional reflexes. The first of these reflexes is evoked by acceleration. The jumper is aided in landing on his feet by the responses to linear acceleration. Responses to rotary acceleration assist gymnasts, dancers, divers, fancy skaters and trapeze performers to maintain balance. Angular acceleration evokes responses in the muscles of the eyes, neck, limbs, and trunk. During rotatary movements the eyes are quickly swung in the direction of the rotation and then slowly swung in the opposite direction. As the rotation continues, these eye movements are repeated. These eye movements are known as nystagmus. When rotation continues at a constant rate, nystagmus gradually fades away indicating that this reaction is due to acceleration and not to velocity. When the rotation is stopped, the head, body, and arms are often turned in the direction of the previous rotation with a resulting loss of balance to that side.

The positional reflex is the reaction that causes the muscles of the neck to keep the head in a normal position regardless of the position of the body. The positional reflex is also responsible for the compensatory deviations of the eyes when the head position is changed.

Reactions from the labyrinth are supplemented by visual and propreoceptive impressions in the maintenance of balance. Overstimulation of the labyrinthine receptors can produce dizziness and nausea. Seasickness is a well known example of this phenomenon. A series of five or more forward rolls down a tumbling mat can produce the same reaction. However, this reaction can be diminished through training. Skilled dancers and figure skaters when doing rapid spins fix their eyes on a distant point and watch that point as long as they can and then quickly turn their head in the direction of the spin and fix their eyes on a new point. This process is repeated throughout the spin. These actions provide a momentary pause in the rotation of the head which reduces the dizziness resulting from overstimulation of the labyrinthine receptors.

The *stretch reflex* is another mechanism which aids in maintaining balance. When a muscle is stretched, receptors in the muscle and its tendon are stimulated and impulses are transmitted to the spinal cord from which impulses travel back to the same muscle causing it to contract reflexly. When an athlete stumbles he "automatically" makes compensatory movements to maintain balance.

PRINCIPLES FOR IMPROVEMENT OF BALANCE

As in improvement of any quality, practice is necessary, progression must be utilized so that the systems involved are challenged, practice should be distributed to eliminate the detrimental influences of fatigue, a variety of balance developing exercises should be practiced and the exercises should be done slowly at first and the speed increased as skill is developed.

Balance Exercises Without Equipment (Static Balance)

1. Stand on toes with feet three inches apart and hold balance for 10 seconds.
2. Number 1 with eyes closed.
3. Balance 10 seconds on one toe and then for 10 seconds on the other toe.
4. Balance on one foot with the eyes closed for 10 seconds.
5. Stand on one foot with eyes closed and rise to stand on one toe. Hold for 10 seconds.
6. Sit on floor with legs raised off floor and hold balance for 10 seconds.
7. *V-Sit.* Sit on floor with legs straight, touch with hands and hold for 5 seconds.
8. *Pelican Stand*—stand on one foot with hands on hips, right foot against left knee, and hold balance for 10 seconds (*Figure 5-1*).
9. *Leg Raise*—stand on the left foot. Grasp the heel of the right foot with the right hand. Extend the right leg and hold balance for 5 seconds.
10. *Front Scale*—stand on the right foot and lower the trunk as you raise your left leg until trunk and left leg form a straight line parallel to the floor. Hold for 5 seconds.

Figure 5-1

11. *Side Scale*—stand on the right foot and lower the trunk to the right as you raise your left leg sideward until the trunk and left leg form a straight line parallel to the floor.

Static Balance Exercise on the Balance Beam

12. Do exercises 7, 8, 9, 10, and 11 on a floor balance beam. Such a beam may be among the school's gymnastics equipment. If it isn't, one can be made by nailing two 2″ x 4″'s ten feet long together and mounting them on a base as illustrated in Diagram 1.

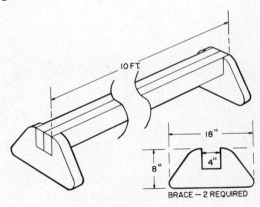

Diagram 1

Balance Exercises without Equipment (Dynamic Balance)

13. Draw 10 circles on the floor 2-1/2 feet apart. The circles should have a diameter of 8 inches. Stand in one of the circles on one toe. Jump from one circle to the next landing on the ball of the opposite foot maintaining balance for 5 seconds without leaving the circle. Continue to all 10 circles.

14. Touch a specific point on the floor with the finger and walk around the point 10 times in 30 seconds while holding the finger in contact with the floor. Then walk a line 10 feet long in 5 seconds.

Dynamic Balance Exercises on the Balance Beam

15. Walk forward across the beam.
16. Walk backward across the beam.
17. Walk forward across the beam on the toes (*Figure 5-2*).
18. Walk backward across the beam on the heels (*Figure 5-3*).
19. Hop forward across the beam.
20. Hop backward across the beam.
21. Hop forward across the beam on one foot.
22. Hop backward across the beam on one foot.
23. Sidestep across the beam (*Figures 5-4 and 5-5*).
24. Sidestep across the beam crossing the right foot in front of and to the left of the left foot, then moving the left foot behind and to the left of the right foot (*Figure 5-6*).
25. Face the length of the beam while standing on one foot and squat while holding the nonsupporting leg extended horizontally forward (*Figure 5-7*).
26. *Cat Walk Forward*—walk the length of the beam forward on both hands and feet (*Figure 5-8*).
27. *Cat Walk Backward*—walk the length of the beam backward on both hands and feet.
28. Do a 180° turn on the balls of the feet.
29. Stand on the beam facing sideward. Leap into the air, do a 180° turn and land in balance facing the opposite direction.
30. Do a 180° turn on the ball of one foot.
31. Do a full turn in the cat walk position.
32. Cat walk sideward across the beam (*Figure 5-9*).
33. Walk across the beam while carrying another athlete "piggy-back" (*Figure 5-10*).

Figure 5-2

Figure 5-3

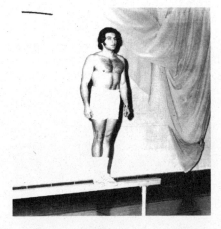

Figure 5-4

Figure 5-5

Figure 5-6

Figure 5-7

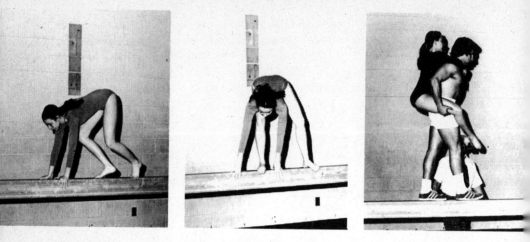

Figure 5-8   **Figure 5-9**   **Figure 5-10**

34. *Wheelbarrow Along Beam*—one athlete places his hands on
the beam while the other, standing on the beam, holds his
legs. The first athlete walks along the beam on his hands
while the other "walks" him forward like a wheelbarrow
(*Figure 5-11*).

35. *Head Wrestling on Beam*—two athletes are on the beam facing one another in cat walk position with heads touching.
They try to push one another off the beam (*Figure 5-12*).

Figure 5-11

Figure 5-12

Dual Combatives for Dynamic Balance

36. *Rooster Fight*—opponents stand in a circle 8 feet in diameter. Each squats and wraps his arms around his legs and grasps his left wrist with his right hand. Opponents endeavor to push one another off balance or out of the circle by bumping each other with their shoulder (*Figure 5-13*).

37. *Indian Hand Wrestle*—opponents stand facing one another with knees and the outside of their right foot in contact with opponent's knee and foot. They grasp right hands and on the signal "Go!" each tries to pull or push the other off balance. If either foot leaves the floor or ground, that athlete loses the contest.

38. *Leg Wrestle*—opponents lie down on their back next to one another with legs running in opposite directions and right hand on opponent's right shoulder. On the count of "one" each raises his right leg vertically. On the count of "two," they repeat this procedure. On the count of "three," they hook legs and each tries to pull his opponent over (*Figure 5-14*).

39. *Horse and Rider*—this combative involves four athletes——two against two. One of each pair "mounts" his partner "piggy back" fashion. Each rider endeavors to grasp the opposing rider and to pull him off his mount or to cause his opponent's mount to lose his balance.

Figure 5-13

Figure 5-14

6

PROCEDURES FOR DEVELOPING ATHLETIC FLEXIBILITY

NATURE OF FLEXIBILITY

Flexibility refers to the range of motion possible in various body joints. A person may have great flexibility in some joints and poor flexibility in other joints. He may, for example, have good flexibility in the hip joint and be very inflexible in the shoulder joint. He may also have good flexibility in one direction and poor flexibility in another direction in the same joint. He may have good flexibility in the hip flexors as manifested by his ability to touch his toes with his hands without bending his knees, while his flexibility in his hip extensors is poor as manifested by his inability to arch his back.

Great strength and great flexibility are not at all incompatible. Many champion weight lifters have been very flexible, being able to do splits and back bends. Strength lies in muscle fibers. Flexibility lies in tendons and ligaments. Anyone can improve his flexibility through stretching exercises done to the point of pain. Some can develop a greater degree of flexibility than others. Skeletal abnormalities or adhesions may limit the range of motion. An increase in flexibility can be effected without decreasing strength.

WHY FLEXIBILITY IS IMPORTANT TO ATHLETES

Athletes in all sports should strive to develop optimal flexibility, because an increase in flexibility of joints decreases the probability of an injury to those joints. With increased flexibility a joint can be flexed or extended to a greater degree before muscles, tendons, or ligaments are torn. When the range of motion has been sufficiently exceeded, there will be an injury. However, that point will not be reached as soon when flexibility has been increased. Increased flexibility of the hamstrings can relieve low back pain. Increased flexibility in the shoulder area can decrease the probability of an athlete suffering torn muscles of the shoulder girdle. Increased flexibility of the ankle joint can decrease the probability of the athlete suffering a sprained ankle.

An improvement in flexibility can result in an improvement in athletic performance. An increase in flexibility permits the athlete to exert force over a greater distance and thereby to generate greater force. For example, greater shoulder flexibility permits the pitcher, discus thrower, passer, javelin thrower, handball player, or tennis player to effect a longer backswing and thereby to increase the distance through which he can increase velocity. The runner can increase the length of his stride by increasing his flexibility. The hurdler can effect a more economical flight since his prime movers don't have to overcome the resistance of tight antagonists. The swimmer's arm recovery in the crawl can be executed with less effort if he has increased flexibility in his shoulder girdle. His kick will be more effective if he has improved his ankle flexibility because his feet will apply thrust through a greater distance in the flutter kick.

DIFFERENCES BETWEEN BALLISTIC AND
STATIC STRETCHING EXERCISES

Stretching exercises are of two types—ballistic and static. In ballistic exercises the momentum of the body or a body part is utilized to stretch the joint. An example is the "toe toucher," in which the athlete starts with his arms raised over his head and swings them downward as he flexes his hips to touch his toes and then swings his arms upward over his head as he extends his hips to come to the erect position. Although ballistic stretching exercises will increase flexibility, there is a possibility of muscle tears if they are done too vigorously. For this reason, static stretching exercises are preferred. In the static stretch, a position of extreme stretch is assumed and held for a period of time. The yogic system makes use of the static stretch. Other examples are the split and backbend done in gymnastics and acrobatic dance.

When the ballistic stretch is done, the athlete should execute the exercise slowly and limit the range of movement. As the circulation is increased and the temperature of the muscle and other tissues is increased, he can increase the speed and intensity of his movements and increase the range of motion. When doing static stretching, he should stretch to the point of some pain. However, if there is some pain the following day, overstretching has probably occurred. It is better to do three sets of ten stretches at three different times during the day than to do them all at once. Stretching exercises should be done every day until the desired range of motion has been achieved. After this, three days per week will be adequate to sustain the degree of flexibility achieved.

PARTNER EXERCISES

Note: The partner pushing or pulling must do so with caution and yet exert force to the tolerance of his partner if maximal improvement in flexibility is to be made. The partner being stretched should not resist the force applied and should let his partner know when his limit has been reached.

1. *Back Pull*—The partner to be stretched lies on his front with his legs spread and his arms extended sideward. His partner sits on his lower back and grasps him under the arms and pulls upward. Hyperextension of thoracic and lumbar spine (*Figure 6-1*).

2. *Assisted Back Bend*—The partner to be stretched lies on her back with her feet drawn up under the buttocks and her hands under her shoulders, fingers pointing toward her feet. The partner stands at her feet facing her, grasps the hips or waist and pulls upward. He may also kneel alongside and facing his partner and lift upward under her waist or hips and place his thigh under her back for additional support. Stretches entire spine and hip extensors (*Figure 6-2*).

Figure 6-1

Figure 6-2

3. *Scale Push*—The partner to be stretched stands with her feet about two feet from the wall or stall bars. She places her hands on the wall or grasps the stall bar with head up; her back is nearly vertical and she raises one leg. The partner stands beside this leg, places one hand just below the knee, grasps the foot with the other hand and pushes downward forward in line with the axis of the bones of this leg. Stretches lumbar spine and hip extensors. Do both legs (*Figure 6-3*).

4. *Scale Bend*—This exercise is similar to the Scale Push except that the trunk of the partner being stretched is almost parallel to the floor. The partner places his shoulder under his foot and pushes forward with his shoulder and left hand while pushing upward and forward with his right hand which is under the partner's knee. Stretches hip extensors, hamstrings, and lumbar spine. Do both legs (*Figure 6-4*).

5. *Quadriceps Stretcher*—The partner to be stretched starts from a kneeling position resting on his lower legs with his toes pointed, his trunk vertical and sitting on his heels. His partner kneels behind him with his hands under his partner's shoulder blades. He assists his partner, if necessary, in lowering his shoulder blades toward and to the floor. Stretches quadriceps and hip extensors.

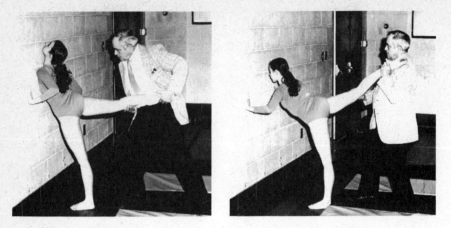

Figure 6-3   **Figure 6-4**

6. *Upper Back Stretcher*—The athlete to be stretched sits on the floor with his legs extended and straddled and his hands clasped behind his head. His partner kneels on one knee behind him and facing him, places the other knee between his shoulder blades, grasps his elbows and while pushing the knee forward pulls his elbows backward. Stretches thoracic spine, anterior deltoids and pectoralis (*Figure 6-5*).

7. *Spine Flexor*—The partner to be stretched sits on the floor with his feet on the floor, knees bent, and his hands clasped behind his head. His partner stands directly behind him and facing him, places her hands on his shoulder blades and pushes downward. Flexion of thoracic and lumbar spine and stretching of hamstrings. A variation of this exercise is done with the legs extended. This places greater stress on the hamstrings and gluteals, but less on the thoracic spine (*Figure 6-6*).

Figure 6-5   **Figure 6-6**

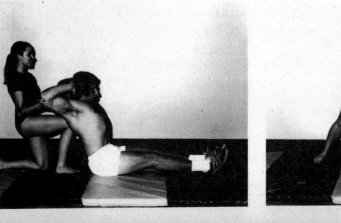

8. *Spine Flexor with Legs Crossed*—This exercise is done in the same manner as the Spine Flexor except that the legs are crossed or the soles of the feet are placed against one another.

9. *The Hook*—The athlete being stretched lies on her back with her arms extended alongside her body, palms down. She elevates her legs and trunk to place her toes on the floor above her head. Her legs are straight and her hips are over her head. Her partner stands between her arms facing the athlete and pushes forward-downward against her hips. Flexion of cervical, thoracic and lumbar spine (*Figure 6-7*).

10. *Praying Mantis*—The athlete sits on the first three inches of a chair with her legs apart and bends forward until her trunk is between her legs. Her partner places one hand on her scapulae and the other on her lower back and pushes downward. Flexion of upper back and hips (*Figure 6-8*).

Figure 6-7   **Figure 6-8**

11. *Sitting Rotor*—The athlete sits on the floor legs straddled and arms extended sideward horizontally. His partner grasps both arms just above the elbow and pulls against one arm while pushing against the other to rotate the athlete's spine. Rotation of thoracic and lumbar spine. Do both directions (*Figure 6-9*).

12. *Opposition Rowing*—Partners sit on the floor facing one another, legs straddled, bottoms of feet against those of partner and hands clasped. Partners alternately lie back to stretch partner and then come through sitting position to be pulled toward the floor. Hip flexion or stretching of hamstrings and gluteals.

Figure 6-9   **Figure 6-10**

13. *Standing Front Split*—The athlete stands with her back to the wall or stall bars. She may hold the stall bars. She raises one leg forward-upward. Her partner stands facing her, grasps the ankle and pushes his partner's leg toward her trunk. Stretches extensor digitorum longus, peroneus longus, brevis, and tertius, plantaris, soleus, tibialis posterior, gastrocnemius, biceps femoris, semitendinosus, semimembranosus, gracilis (hamstrings), and gluteus maximus. Do both legs (*Figure 6-10*).

14. *Torture Rack*—The athlete lies on his front. His partner sits on his upper back, grasps her own hands under her partner's knee and pulls this leg backward. Hyperextension of lumbar spine and hip joint. Stretching of quadricep femoris. Do both legs (*Figure 6-11*).

Figure 6-11   **Figure 6-12**

15. *Lying Assisted Leg Abductor*—The athlete lies on his side and elevates the top leg. His partner stands behind him and facing his side. She grasps her partner's ankle and pulls his leg upward. Stretching of adductors of the hips—pectineus, semimembranosus, semitendinosus, quadratus femoris, adductors longus, magnus, breves and minimus and the gracilis. Do both sides (*Figure 6-12*).

16. *Assisted Quadricep Stretcher*—The athlete lies on his front with one knee bent. His partner grasps his ankle, pushes it toward the athlete's buttocks. Stretches quadriceps. Do both legs (*Figure 6-13*).

17. *Assisted Shoulder Hyperflexor*—The athlete sits on the floor with his legs extended and his arms raised over his head. His partner kneels on one knee behind him, places her other knee between his shoulder blades, grasps his elbows and pulls her partner's arms directly backward. Hyperflexion of the shoulder joint (*Figure 6-14*).

Figure 6-13   **Figure 6-14**

18. *Assisted Shoulder Hyperextensor*—The athlete sits on the floor with his legs extended and straddled and his arms extended downward and backward behind his trunk. His partner stands behind him and facing him, grasps his arms just above the elbow and pulls upward. Hyperextension of the shoulder joint (*Figure 6-15*).

19. *Assisted Shoulder Abductor*—The athlete sits on the floor with his legs extended and straddled and raises his extended arms directly sideward-upward above his head. His arms should be behind his head and his palms should be facing the front. His partner stands behind him, grasps his arms just below the elbows and pushes his arms toward one another. Abduction of the shoulder joint.

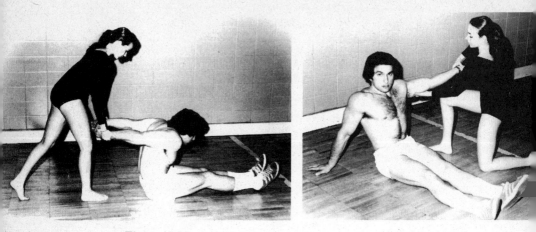

Figure 6-15   **Figure 6-16**

20. *Assisted Outward Rotor*—The athlete sits on the floor with his arm extended sideward. His partner kneels in front of him and grasps his arm just above the elbow with one hand and the hand with her other hand. She rotates the athlete's arm around its mechanical axis so that the thumb of the right hand is turned clockwise. When the left arm is rotated the thumb should be turned counterclockwise. Outward rotation of the shoulder joint. Do both arms (*Figure 6-16*).

21. *Assisted Inward Rotor*—This exercise is done in the same manner as the assisted outward rotor except that the arm is rotated in the opposite direction. Inward rotation of the shoulder joint. Do both arms (*Figure 6-17*).

Figure 6-17   **Figure 6-18**

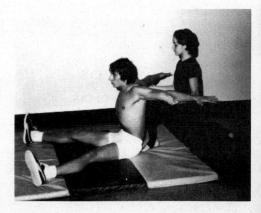

22. *Assisted Horizontal Extensor-Abductor*—The athlete sits on the floor with his legs extended and straddled and his arms extended sideward at shoulder level. His partner stands behind him, grasps his arms at the elbows and exerts a steady pull backward horizontally. Horizontal extension-abduction of the shoulder joint (*Figure 6-18*).

23. *Assited Horizontal Flexor-Adductor*—The athlete sits on the floor, in a chair, or on a bench with his arms extended horizontally forward and crossed. His partner stands behind him, grasps his arms at elbow level and pulls them into a more deeply crossed position, being certain that the arms are at right angles to the trunk through the push. Horizontal flexion-adduction of the shoulder joint (*Figure 6-19*).

24. *Assisted Dorsi Flexor of Feet*—The athlete sits on a chair, bench, or table with the back of his knee on the surface of the chair, bench or table and his feet extended beyond the edge. His partner grasps him behind the heel and places the forearm of this hand against the bottom of the athlete's foot. She applies firm steady pressure to bend the foot backward toward the shin bone. Incidently, this procedure is excellent for relieving cramps in the calf muscles. Stretching of the tendon of achilles. Do both feet (*Figure 6-20*).

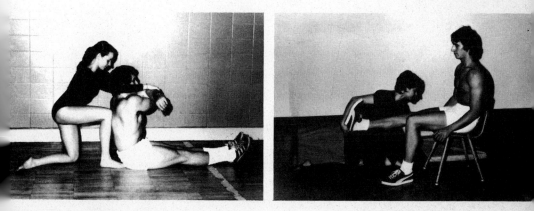

Figure 6-19   **Figure 6-20**

25. *Assisted Plantar Flexor of Feet*—The athlete sits with his legs extended and toes pointed. His partner pushes downward on his instep to increase the degree of plantar flexion or toe point. Stretches muscles on anterior aspect of lower legs and intrinsic muscles on top of the foot.

26. *Assisted Supinator and Pronator of Feet*—These two exercises have been lumped together because the positions of the athlete and his partner are identical in the two exercises. Each exercise, however, is designed to stretch different muscle tendons of the foot. The athlete sits on a bench or table with his feet projecting just beyond the edge. His partner stands facing him and grasps one foot with both hands. She turns the athlete's foot so that the toe is turned inward (adducted) and the medial border is turned upward (inverted) or supinating the foot. She then reverses the direction of the turn so that the foot is pronated, that is, the toe is turned outward (abducted) and the lateral or outer border is turned up (everted). Both ankles should be stretched. The athlete should not resist the stretching but should let his partner know when his tolerance has been reached. The partner should apply slow steady pressure.

If the athlete resists the pressure, the exercises are converted from stretching to isometric exercises which will increase the strength of the muscles supporting the ankle. Improvement in both strength and flexibility of the ankle decreases the probability that the athlete will suffer a sprained ankle—the most common athletic injury (*Figure 6-21*).

INDIVIDUAL EXERCISES

27. *Back Bend*—The athlete lies on her back with her feet drawn up under her buttocks and her hands placed on the floor above her head with the palms down and the fingers pointing toward her feet. She extends her arms and legs to push up into the arched position. If she can get up into a good back bend, she can rock her body back and forth over her hands to increase the stretch in the shoulder joint. Stretching of cervical, thoracic, and lumbar spine, hip and shoulder joints (*Figure 6-22*).

28. *Belly Out*—The athlete stands with his back to the stall bars or a pipe at approximately waist height. He grasps this pipe (or stall bar) behind his body with his palms up and rising on his toes pushes his hips and belly forward until his back is arched as fully as he can tolerate. Stretches shoulder joints, thoracic and lumbar spine and hip joints (quadriceps) (*Figure 6-23*).

29. *Hamstring Stretcher*—The athlete sits on the floor with her legs extended and straddled. She grasps the inner side of each foot and pulls her head as close to the floor as possible holding this position for

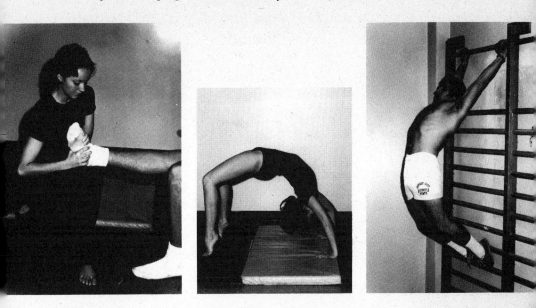

Figure 6-21   **Figure 6-22**   **Figure 6-23**

6 seconds. Stretches the hamstrings and the thoracic and lumbar spine (*Figure 6-24*).

30. *Hurdler's Exercise*—The athlete sits on the floor with one leg extended forward and the other bent and to the side. She grasps her forward leg and pulls her trunk and head as close to her leg (or the floor) as possible and holds this position for 6 seconds. Stretches hip joints and spine (*Figure 6-25*).

31. *Four Point Stretch*—The athlete stands with his palms flat on the floor and his knees bent. He extends his knees as fully as possible while keeping his palms on the floor. Stretches the hamstrings.

A variation of this exercise can be done with the athlete sitting on the floor and holding his insteps with his knees bent. He then extends his knees while continuing to hold his feet.

Figure 6-24   **Figure 6-25**

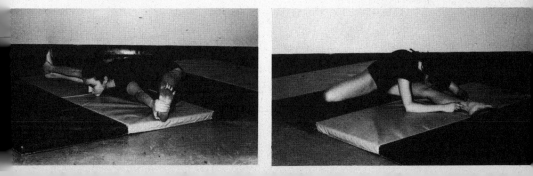

32. *Fore and Aft Split*—The athlete starts in a standing position with one leg extended forward and the other extended backward. She "inches" her feet as far apart as she can (ultimately until her crotch is on the floor with her legs extended). Until she has developed the requisite flexibility, she should lower her body slowly. She can support herself partially on her hands. The stretch should be done with first one leg forward and then the other forward. The position should be held for 6 seconds. Stretches the hip joints, quadriceps, and hamstrings (*Figure 6-26*).

33. *Side Split*—The athlete starts in a standing position with her trunk parallel to the floor, feet straddled and hands on the floor. She slowly "inches" both feet sideward until she is near the limit of her pain tolerance. She should hold this position for 6 seconds. Her ultimate goal should be to lower her crotch to the floor with legs fully extended sideward. Stretches the hip joints (*Figure 6-27*).

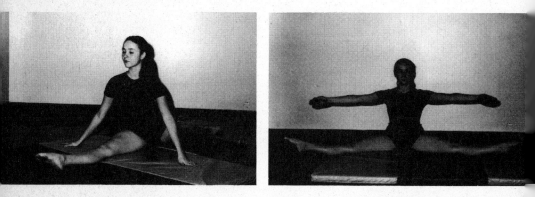

Figure 6-26   **Figure 6-27**

34. *Inch Worm*—The athlete starts in a front leaning rest position (push-up position). Keeping his legs fully extended, he "walks" his feet up between his hands and then "walks" his hands forward to return to the starting position. He should do 5 to 10 repetitions. Stretches the hamstrings and lumbar spine (*Figures 6-28 and 6-29*).

35. *Sitting Rotor*—The athlete is in a sitting position on the floor with her legs bent and soles of the feet against one another. She places both hands on one thigh and pulls with her arms to help pull her trunk toward that side. She holds this position for 6 seconds. She does the same toward the other side. Stretches the spinal rotors (*Figure 6-30*).

Figure 6-28

Figure 6-29

Figure 6-30

Figure 6-31

36. *Shoulder and Hip Stretcher*—The athlete stands facing the stall bars approximately 2 to 3 feet from the stall bars or a pipe which he can grasp. He bends forward at the hips and grasps the pipe and then lowers his trunk as far as his flexibility will allow. He holds this position for 6 seconds. Stretches the hip and shoulder joints.

37. *Sideward V*—The athlete starts standing arms distance from the stall bars and facing them. He grasps the bar at shoulder height, places his feet on the lowest ring and walks his feet up as close to his hands as his flexibility will permit. He holds this position for 6 seconds. Stretches the shoulder and hip joints (*Figure 6-31*).

38. *Hurdler's Stretch*—The athlete assumes the position described in Exercise 30 (Hurdler's Exercise) but instead of bringing her trunk forward, she brings it backward to the floor or as close to it as she can. She holds the position for 6 seconds. She does the exercise to both sides. Stretches the hip joint (*Figure 6-32*).

39. *Hip Stretcher*—The athlete stands with his left side toward the stall bars. He grasps the stall bars with his right hand hand as illustrated. His other hand is on his hip. He pushes his right hip forward-sideward as far as he can and holds the position of maximum stretch for 6 seconds. He does the stretch to both sides (*Figure 6-33*).

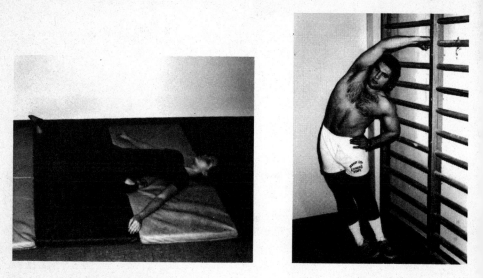

Figure 6-32   **Figure 6-33**

40. *Hip Adductor Stretch*—The athlete is sitting on the floor with the soles of her feet against one another. She pushes downward on both knees holding the position of maximum stretch for 6 seconds. Stretches the hip adductors (*Figure 6-34*).

41. *Trunk Twister*—The athlete starts in a standing position with his feet apart about 18 inches and his arms extended sideward at shoulder height. He swings his trunk downward with a twist to touch his right toe with his left hand at the same time swinging his right arm backward-upward. He returns to the starting position and repeats the movement to the opposite side. He should do 20-30 repetitions. Stretches hips, spinal rotors, shoulders and chest.

| Figure 6-34 | Figure 6-35 | Figure 6-36 |

42. *Standing Rotor*—The athlete starts in a standing position with her feet apart and her arms extended sideward at shoulder height. She rotates her trunk to the right as far as her flexibility will permit and holds this position for 6 seconds. She repeats the exercise to the left. Stretches the spinal rotors (*Figure 6-35*).

43. *Achilles' Stretch*—The athlete stands facing the wall with his hands against it at or lower than shoulder height. He "inches" his feet backward and lowers his body as much as his flexibility will allow while keeping his heels on the floor. He holds this position of maximum stretch for 6 seconds. Stretches the tendon of achilles permitting fuller dorsi flexion (*Figure 6-36*).

44. *Plantar Flexor*—The athlete is in a kneeling position with his toes pointed, trunk erect, and hands on the floor to either side of his thighs. He raises his body supporting his weight on his hands and toes. He should support as large a proportion of his weight on his toes as he can. He holds this position for 6 seconds. Stretches the dorsi flexors of the foot and lower leg to permit a better toe point and a greater range of motion in the direction of plantar flexion resulting in a greater distance through which force is applied in running and jumping (*Figure 6-37*).

45. *The Bouncer*—The athlete starts from a standing position with his feet apart, his hands clasped and his arms extended above his head. He swings his arms downward between his legs as he flexes his

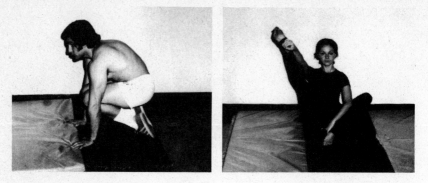

Figure 6-37   **Figure 6-38**

hips and bends his knees and then returns to the starting poisition. He does 20 to 30 repetitions. Stretches the hamstrings and hip extensors.

46. *Sitting Leg Stretcher*—The athlete starts in a sitting position on the floor with her legs bent, the soles of her feet against one another and holding her heels. While continuing to hold her heels, she extends her right leg upward-sideward. She holds this stretch for 6 seconds and then repeats the stretch with the left leg. Stretches the hamstrings and leg adductors. A variation of this exercise is stretching the leg directly forward-upward (*Figure 6-38*).

47. *Side Bender—Side Split*—The athlete starts in a side split. She bends her trunk to the left side and grasps her left ankle with her right hand to bring her head to the floor. She holds this position for 6 seconds and repeats the exercise to the right side. This exercise requires amazing flexibility! Stretches hip adductors to their limit (*Figure 6-39*).

48. *Leg Crossover*—The athlete starts lying on his back with his arms extended sideward at shoulder level. He brings both legs up to his left hand, returns to the starting position and then brings both legs up to his right hand and returns to the starting position. He does 20-25 repetitions. Stretches the hip extensors and rotors of the spine (*Figure 6-40*).

49. *Wrist Exercises*—These exercises, designed to increase range of motion in wrist flexion, extension, ulnar flexion and radial flexion, will all be presented under one heading because of the basic similarity in the procedures. All of these exercises will increase the range of

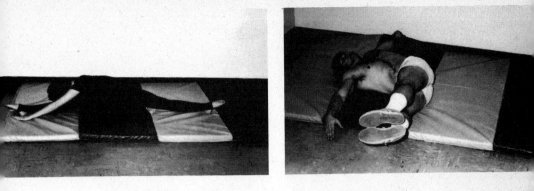

Figure 6-39   **Figure 6-40**

motion of the wrist joint and consequently increase the distance through which force can be applied when throwing a ball, football or javelin, pitching or shot putting.

The athlete places his left hand on the fingertips of his right hand and pushes the fingers toward the forearm until the limit of range of motion has been reached. He holds this position for 6 seconds. He then repeats the exercise for the other hand.

He next pushes on the knuckles of his right hand to force the palm toward the forearm until the limit of the range of motion has been reached. He holds this position for 6 seconds. He repeats the exercise for the other hand.

The athlete pushes on the index finger of his right hand with his left hand until the limits of ulnar flexion have been reached. He holds this position for 6 seconds. He repeats the exercise for his other hand.

Finally, the athlete pushes against his right little finger with his left hand until the limits of radial flexion have been reached. He holds this position for 6 seconds. He repeats the exercise on his other hand.

7

INDIVIDUALIZED EXERCISE PROGRAMS FOR DIFFERENT SPORTS

Few coaches devote adequate time or thought to conditioning programs for their players. Skills must be refined. Strategies must be perfected. Offensive and defensive patterns must be rehearsed. The length of the season is prescribed by conference rules leaving minimal time before the first game. The length of each practice session is delimited by the end of the last class of the day and dinner time. Coaches are often harried, hurried men who have to "milk-out" the maximum good from every second of practice time. Conditioning is left to chance or, at best, receives a minimum of time. Some coaches rationalize that the drills and scrimmage provide all the exercise the players need. This view, however, ignores the physiologic facts.

The coach who dislikes seeing players injured and sidelined cannot ignore conditioning because a conditioning program will decrease the incidence of injuries. Stronger muscles give greater stability to joints and thereby decrease the probability of a sprain or dislocation. Stronger muscles provide more cushioning soft tissue over bones and thereby decrease the probability of a fracture. Flexible ligaments and tendons can be stretched farther before tearing.

Coaches who enjoy winning cannot ignore conditioning. The first step in preparing players for the season's games is conditioning. Condition is basic and prerequisite to the development of maximal skill. The player who is thoroughly fatigued by the third quarter cannot perform at his highest skill during the second half. Timing, coordination, balance, power, agility, and strength decline when fatigue sets in. Passes are missed. Foul shots are missed. Kicks are misdirected. Furthermore, fatigue increases the possibility of an injury.

Players with insufficient strength cannot push their opponent out of the way, or pull a rebound out of the opponent's hands or kick or throw as far as they might. They cannot run as fast, dodge as quickly, jump as high or hit as hard as they could if they were stronger.

Flexible players can take a longer backswing, plantar flex their foot farther and flex or hyperextend their hip farther and consequently can apply thrust against the racquet, ball, javelin, or ground for a greater distance to get more distance or speed. Flexible wrestlers can effect an escape more easily.

Studies have shown that players' physical fitness level depreciates during the season. Participation in a sport will develop only the level of strength, endurance, power, and flexibility necessary to get through the game. To secure maximal improvement in these qualities, the overload principle must be made operative. This means that as condition improves, the load must be constantly increased. This cannot be done in scrimmage, drills, or a game. It must be done through an exercise program in which the dosage can be measured and controlled.

Even though the practice time is limited and there is much to be accomplished, there is no excuse for fielding a team which has not been maximally conditioned. Players can be given an individualized conditioning program to conduct on their own for three months previous to the first practice session. This program should be written out for the player. The player should be instructed to report to practice having achieved a stipulated (and reasonable) level of improvement.

A conditioning class could be established for the players (and other interested students). This class could meet five days per week for the fifteen weeks previous to the first practice session. Obviously, there could be no work on the skills or strategies of the game during these classes. If conference officials have concern for the health and safety of the players, they could not object, since this conditioning program would decrease the incidence of injuries.

In recognition that practice time is limited and since each sport skill requires strength, power, or flexibility in different areas, the author has developed a specialized conditioning program for the different positions in sports and for different sports. Participants in all sports need all the qualities of physical fitness but in some sports leg power is of greatest importance. In others, upper body strength is of greatest importance. In some, flexibility is of great importance. In the design of these exercise programs and the selection of the exercises, it was necessary to make a kinesiologic analysis of the skills to determine which muscles are involved as prime movers, antagonists, assistors and stabilizers and to determine which muscles needed to be strengthened and which stretched. It was necessary to determine the relative amount of aerobic and anaerobic endurance to be developed. The exercises are listed by number as they appear in the text. The first number indicates the chapter and the second number indicates the number of the exercise in the chapter.

FOOTBALL LINEMEN

An offensive lineman starts from a three-point stance with his feet spread, one foot slightly forward of the other and his knees and hips flexed. When the ball is snapped, he must react with speed and power. He plantar flexes his feet, extends his knees and hips, hyperextends his spine and neck, flexes his elbows and abducts his arms to smash his arms and shoulders into the defensive lineman and also to broaden his base of contact. The effectiveness of his efforts depend primarily upon mass (weight) and power.

The lineman can add functional mass and develop power through strength building exercises. The areas where power is of greatest importance are in the plantar flexors of the feet, knee, and hip extensors, spinal hyperextenders, neck, elbow flexors and arm abductors (shoulder area). To stabilize body parts, he also needs strong leg adductors, knee and hip flexors, spinal flexors, and shoulder horizontal adductors.

In order to provide thrust over a greater distance, he needs flexibility in the ankle joint (both plantar and dorsal flexion), knee joint (hamstrings), hip joint flexion and spinal flexion. He needs to stretch these muscles groups.

He needs muscular endurance and anaerobic endurance since each play takes 10-15 seconds followed by a 10-20 second rest. Consequently, he should do a good deal of interval training as well as muscular endurance work for the muscles involved.

Initial tests will provide the coach with clues as to the number of repetitions and the load with which the athlete should begin his conditioning program. Dosages should be increased sufficiently to provide the athlete with continually increasing challenge. The stretching exercises should be done three times each day, six days per week but only after some warm-up exercises. The strength, muscular endurance, and cardiovascular/respiratory endurance exercises should be done four times per week.

CONDITIONING EXERCISES FOR
OFFENSIVE FOOTBALL LINEMEN

Strength Exercises

Exercises for arms and shoulder girdle (4-6 repetitions, 4-5 sets each), 75% of maximum):

1-1	Military press
1-2	Press behind neck
1-3	Seated military press
1-4	Bench press
1-5	Bent over rowing
1-6	Upright rowing
1-7	Front curl

Exercises for Legs and Feet

1-15	Dead lift
1-16	Power clean
1-17	Dead hang power clean
1-18	Squat
1-19	Front squat
1-20	Back squat
1-21	Rise on toes
1-22	Leg curl
1-23	Knee extensor

Exercises for trunk and neck

1-24	Shoulder shrug
1-25	Lateral rise with dumbells
1-26	Forward rise with dumbells
1-27	Supine lateral dumbell rise
1-29	Good morning exercise
1-30	Sit up
1-31	Neck flexor

Strength Exercises with the Isometric Belt for Offensive Linemen

If the athlete or coach prefers, the same improvement in strength can be secured in less than one-third the time per workout through use of the isometric belt. These exercises follow:

Exercises for the arms and shoulders girdle

2-1	Military press
2-2	Press behind neck
2-3	Supine press
2-5	Front curl
2-6	Reverse curl
2-7	Standing pull-up
2-9	Forward extended arm elevator
2-11	Sideward extended arm elevator
2-18	Rower's exercise

Exercises for the trunk and neck

2-21	Forward push—neck
2-22	Backward push—neck
2-23	Sideward push—neck
2-24	Head turn—neck
2-25	Front shoulder shrug
2-26	Back shoulder shrug
2-29	Supine extended arm elevator
2-30	Bent over rowing exercise
2-31	Dead lift
2-32	Suitcase lift

Exercises for the legs and feet

2-33	Squat
2-34	Sitting leg extensor
2-35	Prone leg extensor

2-36	Supine hip flexor
2-38	Sitting leg adductor
2-39	Side leg flexor
2-40	Side leg extensor
2-41	Sitting leg raiser
2-42	Rise on toes
2-43	Sitting plantar flexor

Isometric Exercises with a Beach Towel, a Partner, or Items in the Home for Offensive Linemen

If the lineman wishes to do the isometric exercises but no belt is available, he can use a beach towel, items in the home, or a partner. These exercises follow:

Exercises for arms and shoulder girdle

3-1	Military press
3-2	Press behind neck
3-3	Supine press
3-5	Front curl
3-6	Reverse curl
3-7	Standing pull-up
3-10	Forward extended arm elevator
3-11	Sideward extended arm elevator

Exercises for legs and feet

3-14	Sitting leg extensor
3-15	Sitting plantar flexor
3-16	Prone leg extensor
3-17	Supine hip flexor
3-19	Sitting foot abductor
3-20	Side leg flexor
3-21	Side leg extensor
3-22	Sitting leg adductor

Exercises for trunk and neck

3-27	Head backward push
3-28	Head sideward push
3-29	Head turn
3-30	Supine extended arm elevator
3-32	Bent over rowing exercise
3-33	Dead lift
3-34	Suitcase lift

Following are isometric exercises which the offensive lineman can do in his home:

Exercises for the arms and shoulder girdle

3-37	Extended arm elevator
3-39	Flexed arm elevator
3-42	Arm extensor
3-43	Front curl on a desk
3-44	Reverse curl on a desk
3-47	Chair lift
3-48	Parade rest pull
3-50	Sideward arm elevator
3-52	Forward extended arm elevator
3-54	Resisted push-up

Exercises for the legs and feet

3-55	Sitting knee extensor
3-56	Sitting leg adductor
3-58	Dorsi-flexor on desk
3-61	Rise on toes on door frame
3-62	Sitting knee extensor with partner
3-63	Sitting knee flexor with partner

Exercises for the trunk and neck

3-67	Neck exercises
3-68	Seated dead lift
3-69	Seated shoulder shrug
3-70	Sit-up with a partner
3-71	Prone back arch with partner
3-72	Prone leg curl with a partner

In all four strength programs (progressive resistance exercises, use of the isometric belt, isometric exercises with a towel or isometric exercises without equipment), the athlete should do an exercise for the arms and shoulder girdle, then one for the legs and feet, then one for the trunk and neck—doing an exercise for one part of the body and then for another until he has progressed through the entire series.

ENDURANCE EXERCISES FOR THE LINEMAN

The coach or one of his assistants should lead the linemen in grass drills of twenty ten-second bouts. These should be done at the end of the practice session. Grass drills should be followed by wind sprints over four lengths of the field with a distance of 10 to 20 yards between whistles. The coach or his assistant could also lead the linemen in rope skipping. Ten to 20 bouts of rope skipping of 150-250 turns of the rope with a 30-60 second rest between bouts should be done.

If the linemen are conditioning on their own, the coach can establish a circuit training course for the athletes. They can follow Cureton's Progressive, Rhythmical, Nonstop Exercise program building up to at least Lesson XV—High Gear, or they can do cycling for anaerobic power alternately sprinting all-out for one-quarter of a mile and then peddling slowly for one-quarter of a mile. If the coach decides to establish a circuit training course, it should emphasize development of strength, muscular endurance and flexibility in those areas alluded to earlier. The activity should be intensive but of short duration. The sample circuit presented in the text on page 106 is a good one for football linemen if dead lifts are substituted for the side straddle hops and the supine press for the lateral run.

Balance Exercises for Offensive Linemen

A lineman needs good dynamic balance because he is useless when he is on his back. All of the dual combatives described in Chapter 5 are recommended for the linemen.

Flexibility Exercises for Offensive Linemen

Offensive linemen are notoriously inflexible. While great demands are not placed upon them for flexibility, they will become more effective and suffer fewer injuries if they practice the following exercises:

6-5	Quadriceps stretcher
6-7	Spine flexor
6-9	The hook
6-10	Praying mantis
6-12	Opposition rowing
6-16	Assisted quadricep stretcher
6-24	Assisted dorsi flexor of feet
6-25	Assisted plantar flexor of feet
6-29	Hamstring stretcher
6-30	Hurdler's exercise
6-31	Four point stretch
6-34	Inch worm
6-36	Shoulder and hip stretcher

6-37	Sideward V
6-41	Trunk twister
6-43	Achilles stretch
6-44	Plantar flexor
6-45	The bouncer
6-48	Leg crossover

EXERCISES FOR DEFENSIVE LINEMEN

The defensive lineman has basically the same conditioning needs as does the offensive lineman. However, he has some additional needs. He is permitted to use his hands to pull or push the offensive lineman. He pushes or pulls sideward as well as forward. This mandates that he possess strength and power in the lateral and rotary direction as well as forward. He needs more strength in the elbow extensors for the forearm shiver and more strength to elevate the arms forward (flexion) to smash his arms into the chest of the offensive lineman. He also needs more flexibility since if he can "give," he'll be more difficult to block.

The defensive lineman should substitute the following listed exercises for those listed:

Strength Exercises

Exercises eliminated

1-5	Bent over rowing
1-6	Upright rowing
1-25	Lateral rise with dumbbells
1-26	Forward rise with dumbbells
2-7	Standing pull-up
2-26	Back shoulder shrug
3-71	Prone back arch with partner

Exercises substituted

1-13	Front wrist curl
1-14	Reverse wrist curl
2-4	Arm depressor
2-8	Forward extended arm depressor
2-9	Forward extended arm elevator
2-10	Sideward extended arm depressor
2-13	Bowler's exercise
2-17	Swimmer's exercise
2-17	Butterfly swimmer's exercise

2-20	Wrist and forearm exercise
2-20	Wrist front curl
2-20	Wrist reverse curl
2-27	Chest pull
2-28	Chest push
3-25	Chest pull (towel)
3-35	Wrist front curl
3-36	Wrist reverse curl
3-45	Arm depressor on desk
3-76	Wrist pronator and supinator

Flexibility Exercises

The defensive lineman should follow the same program as the offensive lineman for endurance and balance. However, since the rules permit the defensive lineman greater freedom in movement, he will need to do the following additional flexibility exercises:

5-1	Back pull
5-6	Upper back stretcher
5-11	Sitting rotar (assisted)
5-35	Sitting rotar (unassisted)
5-42	Standing rotar

FOOTBALL OFFENSIVE BACKFIELD

Offensive backfield players suffer a high incidence of sprains of the ankle and knee. Speed is of greater importance to them than it is to linemen. For these reasons, they need to do more stretching exercises for the ankle and knee and more strength building exercises for the ankle. They need good flexibility in the hip joint to evade tacklers. They also need more aerobic and anaerobic power than do linemen. Since they pass and kick the ball they need more wrist and hip flexibility. They also need a higher level of dynamic balance. For these reasons, it is recommended that offensive backfield players substitute the following exercises for those listed below:

Exercises eliminated

1-24	Shoulder shrug
1-27	Supine lateral dumbell rise
2-25	Front shoulder shrug
2-26	Back shoulder shrug
2-29	Supine extended arm elevator

2-30	Bent over rowing exercise
3-7	Standing pull-up
3-10	Forward extended arm elevator
3-11	Sideward extended arm elevator
3-30	Supine extended arm elevator
3-32	Bent over rowing exercise
3-37	Extended arm elevator
3-47	Chair lift
3-69	Seated shoulder shrug

Exercises substituted

1-8	Reverse curl
1-10	Triceps exercise
1-11	Supine triceps extension
1-12	Bent arm pull-over
2-14	Javelin thrower's exercise
2-37	Sitting leg abductor
2-44	Sitting dorsal flexor
2-45	Sitting foot abductor
2-46	Sitting foot abductor
2-37	Sitting leg abductor
2-45	Sitting foot abductor
2-44	Sitting dorsal flexor
3-31	Pull over
3-46	Arm depressor on chair
3-53	Pull over
3-57	Sitting leg abductor
3-59	Foot abductor
3-60	Foot adductor
3-64	Ankle eversion and inversion with partner

Endurance Exercises for Offensive Backfield

Offensive backfield players need excellent anaerobic power and good aerobic power. They should be able to sprint 100 yards in full uniform in a time which is competitive in track. The interval training technique described in Chapter 4, page 115 should be applied to a sprint of 150 yards (most running in football is broken field running). The beginning distance should be 50 yards progressing by increments of 25 yards to 150 yards. The time at each distance (50, 75, 100, and 125 yards) should be progressively decreased until the athlete can run 150 yards in the time established as the goal.

On his own time, out of season, the athlete should practice Cooper's aerobics or do cycling. He could do rope skipping, wind sprints, grass drills, and Cureton's program with the entire squad.

Flexibility Exercises for Offensive Backfield

Offensive backfield players should do all the exercises listed for both defensive and offensive linemen plus the following exercises:

6-15	Lying assisted leg abductor
6-17	Assisted shoulder hyperflexor
6-19	Assisted shoulder abductor
6-22	Assisted horizontal extensor-abductor
6-26	Assisted supinator and pronator of feet
6-36	Shoulder and hip stretcher
6-39	Hip abductor stretch
6-49	Wrist exercises

BASKETBALL

Basketball players need both aerobic and anaerobic power. They need strong plantar flexors, knee, hip, and spine extensors and shoulder muscles to leap high for lay-up shots, basket defense and to recover rebounds. To recover rebounds they also need strong hands and arm flexors. Since the incidence of sprains of the ankle joint is relatively high among basketball players, they need to strengthen and increase the flexibility of the ankle joint.

CONDITIONING EXERCISES FOR BASKETBALL PLAYERS

Strength Exercises

Progressive resistance exercises

Use 50% of maximum weight which can be lifted in each exercise. Do 15-20 repetitions in each of 2-3 sets.

Exercises for arms and shoulder girdle

1-1	Military press
1-7	Front curl
1-8	Reverse curl
1-9	Lateral exercise
1-10	Triceps exercise
1-12	Bent arm pull-over
1-13	Front wrist curl
1-14	Reverse wrist curl

Exercises for legs and feet

1-15	Dead lift
1-18	Squat
1-19	Front squat
1-20	Back squat
1-21	Rise on toes
1-23	Knee extensor

Exercises for trunk and neck

1-25	Forward rise with dumbbells
1-29	Good morning exercise

Exercises with the isometric belt

Exercises for the arms and shoulder girdle

2-1	Military press
2-3	Supine press
2-5	Front curl
2-6	Reverse curl
2-20	Wrist and forearm exercise
2-29	Supine extended arm elevator

Exercises for the back and trunk

2-31	Dead lift

Exercises for the legs and feet

2-9	Forward extended arm elevator
2-18	Rower's exercise
2-33	Squat
2-34	Sitting leg extensor
2-35	Prone leg extensor
2-36	Supine hip flexor
2-40	Side leg extensor
2-42	Rise on toes
2-43	Sitting plantar flexor
2-44	Sitting dorsal flexor
2-45	Sitting foot adductor
2-46	Sitting foot abductor

Isometric exercises with a towel

Exercises for the arms and shoulder girdle

3-1	Military press
3-3	Supine press

3-5   Front curl
3-6   Reverse curl
3-10   Forward extended arm elevator

Exercises for the legs and feet

3-14   Sitting leg extensor
3-15   Sitting plantar flexor
3-16   Prone leg extensor
3-19   Sitting foot abductor
3-21   Side leg extensor
3-23   Sitting foot adductor
3-24   Sitting dorsi flexor

Exercises for the trunk

3-30   Supine extended arm elevator
3-33   Dead lift

Exercises for the wrists and hands

3-35   Wrist front curl
3-36   Wrist reverse curl

Isometric exercises without equipment

Exercises for the arms and shoulder girdle

3-37   Extended arm elevator
3-40   Flexed arm depressor
3-42   Arm extensor
3-43   Front curl on a desk
3-44   Reverse curl on a desk
3-46   Arm depressor on a chair
3-52   Forward extended arm elevator

Exercises for the legs and feet

3-55   Sitting knee extensor
3-58   Dorsi-flexor on desk
3-59   Foot abductor
3-60   Foot adductor
3-61   Rise on toes in door frame
3-62   Sitting knee extensor with partner
3-64   Ankle eversion and inversion with partner

Exercises for the trunk

3-68   Seated dead lift

Exercises for the wrists and hands

3-74   Wrist front curl
3-75   Wrist reverse curl
3-76   Wrist pronator and supinator
3-78   Seated finger flexor and extensor against desk

ENDURANCE EXERCISES FOR BASKETBALL PLAYERS

Basketball players need both aerobic and anaerobic power. Play is continuous and fast moving during the twenty minute halves for college players and fifteen minute halves for high school players. The court is between 24-2/3 and 31 yards in length. Consequently, sprints are short. However, the rest period between movement from one end of the court to the other is extremely brief. Endurance conditioning programs for basketball players should be structured to consist of intensive work for three seconds followed by slow paced work for two seconds repeated twelve times per minute and continued at this pace for up to fifteen minutes. It is not surprising that basketball players are all lean.

Grass drills and wind sprints serve this purpose admirably. Grass drills could be done intensively for three seconds followed by two seconds of slow easy jogging in place barely picking up the feet for two seconds. Twelve such bouts per minute for eight minutes could be the starting point building up to fifteen minutes by the end of the conditioning period.

If the choice of conditioning procedure is wind sprints, the players could sprint the length of the basketball court, rest two seconds and sprint across again for a total of nine sprints per minute for ten minutes at the beginning of the conditioning program, and building up to fifteen minutes.

If the choice is rope skipping, the players should skip at their fastest rate for five seconds and then skip slowly for three seconds repeating these bouts seven or eight times per minute for ten minutes for a total of seventy or eighty bouts.

On their own time, the players could practice Cooper's aerobics.

FLEXIBILITY FOR BASKETBALL PLAYERS

Basketball players need a fairly high degree of flexibility in many joints. Since they suffer a high incidence of ankle injuries, they need to develop flexibility in the ankle joint along with strength to decrease the probability of an ankle injury. They also need flexibility in this joint, particularly in the direction of plantar flexion, in order to provide thrust over a greater distance to increase the height of their jump. They need flexibility in the hamstrings in order that the quadriceps won't have to work against the resistance of tight hamstrings when leaping. They need good shoulder flexibility when struggling to get rebounds if the ball is behind their body. They need good spinal rotation after they get a rebound in order to twist away from opponents.

6-5	Quadriceps stretcher
6-6	Upper back stretcher
6-7	Spine flexor
6-9	The hook
6-10	Praying mantis
6-11	Sitting rotor
6-12	Opposition rowing
6-16	Assisted quadricep stretcher
6-17	Assisted shoulder hyperflexor
6-19	Assisted shoulder abductor
6-22	Assisted horizontal extensor-abductor
6-24	Assisted dorsi-flexor of feet
6-25	Assisted plantor-flexor of feet
6-26	Assisted supinator and pronator of feet
6-29	Hamstring stretcher
6-30	Hurdler's exercise
6-31	Four point stretch
6-34	Inch worm
6-35	Sitting rotar
6-36	Shoulder and hip stretcher
6-37	Sideward V
6-41	Trunk twister
6-42	Standing rotar
6-43	Achilles stretch
6-44	Plantar flexor
6-45	The bouncer
6-48	Leg crossover
6-49	Wrist exercises

AGILITY FOR BASKETBALL PLAYERS

Anyone who does not appreciate the importance of agility in the game of basketball has never seen a basketball game. Agility is the most important physical fitness quality in basketball. As we have pointed out earlier, development of strength, flexibility, dynamic balance and skill will enhance agility. However, it is advisable to incorporate agility drills early in the practice sessions. Players could dribble back and forth and sideward against time between two lines twenty feet apart. They could dribble around obstacles or around one another.

CONDITIONING FOR BASEBALL

Baseball players need strong legs, spinal rotars, shoulders, arms and wrists to swat home runs and to pitch and to throw balls from the outfield. They also need flexible wrists, shoulders, hips and spinal rotars to do these skills at maximum efficiency. They need flexible hips to snag grounders. Demands upon cardio-respiratory endurance are not great during a baseball game; however, baseball players should do endurance work in order to avoid fatigue during a game. Reflexes, coordination and timing, so crucial in baseball, are the first affected when fatigue begins to set in.

Strength Exercises for Baseball Players

Use 50% of maximum weight which can be lifted in each exercise. Do 15-20 repetitions in each of 2-3 sets.

Exercises with barbells

1-1	Military press
1-2	Press behind neck
1-4	Bench press
1-7	Front curl
1-8	Reverse curl
1-10	Triceps exercise
1-11	Supine triceps extension
1-13	Front wrist curl
1-14	Reverse wrist curl
1-18	Squat
1-19	Front squat
1-20	Back squat
1-21	Rise on toes
1-22	Leg curl
1-28	Standing dumbbell swing
1-30	Sit-up

Isometric exercise

2-1	Military press
2-2	Press behind neck

2-3	Supine press
2-8	Forward extended arm depressor
2-10	Sideward extended arm depressor
2-14	Javelin thrower's exercise
2-20	Wrist and forearm exercise
2-32	Suitcase lift
2-33	Squat
2-34	Sitting leg extensor
2-38	Sitting leg adductor
2-42	Rise on toes
2-43	Sitting plantar flexor

Isometric exercises with a beach towel

3-1	Military press
3-2	Press behind neck
3-3	Supine press
3-8	Forward extended arm depressor
3-9	Sideward extended arm depressor
3-13	Swimmer's exercise
3-14	Sitting leg extensor
3-15	Sitting plantar flexor
3-31	Pull-over
3-34	Suitcase lift
3-35	Wrist front curl
3-36	Wrist reverse curl

Isometric exercises without equipment

3-38	Extended arm depressor
3-40	Flexed arm depressor
3-42	Arm extensor
3-45	Arm depressor on desk
3-46	Arm depressor on chair
3-49	Overhead pull
3-51	Sideward arm depressor
3-53	Pull-over
3-55	Sitting knee extensor
3-61	Rise on toes in door frame
3-62	Sitting knee extensor with partner
3-74	Wrist front curl
3-75	Wrist reverse curl
3-76	Wrist pronator and supinator
3-77	Fist clenching and squeezing a rubber ball
3-78	Seated finger flexor and extensor against a desk

Endurance Exercises for Baseball Players

Demands upon endurance in baseball are minimal. Short sprints when going after balls or while running bases are the extent of sustained movement. For this reason, baseball players should do wind sprints covering short distances between whistles, grass drills of short duration (20 ten second bouts with ten second rest periods between bouts) and rope skipping (20 thirty second bouts with rest periods of thirty seconds between bouts).

Although it is true that baseball places little demand upon endurance, baseball players should do some aerobic work in order to keep over-all physical fitness at a high level in order to minimize decrements in timing, speed and power which might occur by the ninth inning of a game. For this reason, well conditioned baseball players should jog a mile or more each day at the close of practice.

Agility Exercises for Baseball Players

Baseball players demonstrate a high degree of agility in scooping up a grounder and throwing to first base, in catching a throw from third base and pivoting to tag the runner on second, in sliding into home plate, in stealing a base and in many other skills peculiar to baseball. In addition to the agility inherent in these movements, a high degree of skill is required to catch the ball and to throw it with accuracy and speed. Skill in throwing and catching is best acquired through practice in throwing and catching. Many hours of practice are required. The agility factor is most easily and economically acquired while practicing the entire movement pattern.

Balance Exercises for Baseball Players

The game of baseball requires a high degree of dynamic balance. The baseball player must maintain balance while receiving the impact of the ball in his glove and while giving impetus to the ball when batting or throwing. However, as with agility, maintenance of balance is highly related to the skill. Consequently, balance is best developed while practicing the skills of baseball.

Flexibility Exercises for Baseball Players

Baseball players need good hamstring and hip flexibility in order to scoop up grounders effortlessly. They need good wrist and shoulder flexibility and good range of movement in spinal and shoulder rotation in order to provide thrust through a greater range while batting and throwing. For these reasons, flexibility exercises have been selected which will increase the range of motion in the wrists, shoulders and hips and which will facilitate spinal and shoulder rotation.

Partner exercises

6-6	Upper back stretcher
6-7	Spine flexor
6-8	Spine flexor with leg crossed
6-9	The hook
6-10	Praying mantis
6-11	Sitting rotar
6-17	Assisted shoulder hyper flexor
6-18	Assisted shoulder hyper extensor
6-20	Assisted outward rotar
6-21	Assisted inward rotar
6-22	Assisted horizontal extensor-abductor
6-25	Assisted plantar-flexor of feet

Individual exercises

6-29	Hamstring stretcher
6-30	Hurdler's exercise
6-31	Four point stretch
6-34	Inch worm
6-35	Sitting rotar
6-37	Sideward V
6-38	Hurdler's stretch
6-41	Trunk twister
6-42	Standing rotar
6-44	Plantar flexor
6-45	The bouncer
6-46	Sitting leg stretch
6-48	Leg crossover
6-49	Wrist exercises

CONDITIONING EXERCISES FOR TENNIS, BADMINTON, SQUASH, PADDLEBALL AND HANDBALL

The dual court games of tennis, badminton, squash, paddleball and handball, have certain characteristics in common which provide mandates for conditioning programs. All of these games require power in the muscles of the shoulders and wrists. Consequently, exercises to develop strength in the muscles of the shoulder, arms and upper trunk are required. All of these games require anaerobic power. Short bursts of intense activity alternate with short rest periods. Consequently, exercises are presented which develop this kind of cardiovascular, respiratory fitness. All of these games demand essentially the same kind of agility—short runs with quick changes of direction. All of these games make about the same demands upon flexibility.

Strength Exercises

Progressive resistance exercises: (Use a weight with which you can do 15-20 repetitions in each of 2-3 sets.) Use 50% of maximum weight able to lift in each exercise.

1-1	Military press
1-2	Press behind neck
1-3	Seated military press
1-4	Bench press
1-7	Front curl
1-8	Reverse curl
1-10	Triceps exercise
1-11	Supine triceps extension
1-12	Bent arm pull-over
1-13	Front wrist curl
1-14	Reverse wrist curl
1-21	Rise on toes
1-24	Shoulder shrug
1-25	Lateral rise with dumbbells
1-27	Supine lateral dumbbell rise

Isometric exercises with the isometric belt

2-1	Military press
2-2	Press behind neck
2-3	Supine press
2-4	Arm depressor
2-5	Front curl
2-6	Reverse curl
2-7	Standing pull-up
2-8	Forward extended arm depressor
2-9	Forward extended arm elevator
2-10	Sideward extended arm depressor
2-11	Sideward extended arm elevator
2-13	Bowler's exercise

2-20	Wrist and forearm exercise
2-25	Front shoulder shrug
2-26	Back shoulder shrug
2-27	Chest pull
2-28	Chest push
2-30	Bent over rowing exercise
2-32	Suitcase lift

Isometric exercises with a beach towel

3-1	Military press
3-2	Press behind neck
3-3	Supine press
3-4	Arm depressor
3-5	Front curl
3-6	Reverse curl
3-8	Forward extended arm depressor
3-9	Sideward extended arm depressor
3-10	Forward extended arm elevator
3-11	Sideward extended arm elevator
3-25	Chest pull
3-30	Supine extended arm elevator
3-31	Pull-over
3-32	Bent over rowing exercise
3-34	Suitcase lift
3-35	Wrist front curl
3-36	Wrist reverse curl

Isometric exercises without equipment

3-37	Extended arm elevator
3-38	Extended arm depressor
3-39	Flexed arm elevator
3-40	Flexed arm depressor
3-41	Forward extended arm sideward mover
3-42	Arm extensor
3-43	Front curl on a desk
3-44	Reverse curl on a desk
3-45	Arm depressor on a desk
3-46	Arm depressor on chair
3-47	Chair lift
3-48	Parade rest pull
3-50	Sideward arm elevator
3-51	Sideward arm depressor

3-52	Forward extended arm elevator
3-53	Pull-over
3-54	Resisted push-up
3-65	Chest push
3-66	Chest pull
3-69	Seated shoulder shrug
3-74	Wrist front curl
3-75	Wrist reverse curl
3-76	Wrist pronator and supinator
3-77	Fist clenching
3-78	Seated finger flexor and extensor against a desk

Endurance and Agility Exercises for Tennis, Badminton, Squash, Paddleball and Handball

Court games place their greatest demand upon anaerobic fitness since bursts of intensive activity alternate (after moving back to the key position) with a brief rest period while waiting for the ball or shuttlecock to be returned. The activity is not sustained at a uniform but relatively slow pace as in distance running, swimming, cycling or cross country skiing. Consequently, these games call for interval type conditioning.

The ability to move quickly from one spot to another, or agility, is a very important quality required for these games as is anaerobic power.

A drill utilizing half of a basketball, tennis or badminton court or a handball court is suggested. Let's call this drill "clock dodge." Numbers are placed on the floor and a circle with a diameter of one foot is painted in the center as indicated in Diagram 2. The player begins standing in the center circle. The coach calls numbers 1 through 8 in random order. The player runs to the number called and back to the center circle as rapidly as he can. As soon as the player returns to the center circle, the coach calls another number. The player must at all times face the front (number 1). He may back pedal or sidestep to reach any number. The score is the number of times he returns to the center circle in one minute. Half scores may be counted.

Grass drills could be done intensively for 3 seconds followed by a one-second rest. Fifteen such bouts per minute for 8 minutes could be the starting point building up to 15 minutes by the end of the conditioning season.

If the choice of conditioning procedure is wind sprints, the player should sprint 30 feet, rest for one second and sprint again for a total of

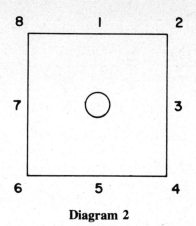

Diagram 2

roughly 15 sprints per minute. The sprints should be continued for 5 to 6 minutes building up to 10 minutes by the end of the conditioning season.

If the choice of conditioning procedure is rope skipping, the players should skip at their fastest rate for 5 seconds and then rest for 3 seconds, repeating these bouts 7 or 8 times per minute for 5 to 6 minutes. This dosage should be increased to 10 minutes by the end of the conditioning season.

Balance for Tennis, Badminton, Squash, Paddleball and Handball Players

These players must maintain balance after checking the momentum gained in a short fast run and while swinging at the ball or shuttlecock. Balance is a factor in agility and will be developed in the agility drills, in the "clock dodge" described earlier and while playing the game. For these reasons, we will present no balance drills.

Flexibility Exercises for Tennis, Badminton, Squash, Paddleball and Handball Players

These players need good shoulder and wrist flexibility and a good range of motion in spinal rotation in order to provide thrust against the ball or shuttlecock through a greater range.

Partner exercises

6-1	Sitting rotar
6-17	Assisted shoulder hyperflexor
6-18	Assisted shoulder hyperextensor

6-19   Assisted shoulder abductor
6-20   Assisted outward rotar
6-21   Assisted inward rotar
6-22   Assisted horizontal extensor abductor
6-23   Assisted horizontal flexor abductor

Individual exercises

6-35   Sitting rotar
6-36   Shoulder and hip stretcher
6-39   Hip abductor stretch
6-41   Trunk twister
6-42   Standing rotar
6-48   Leg crossover
6-49   Wrist exercises

CONDITIONING EXERCISES FOR GYMNASTS

Anyone who has ever watched a championship gymnastic meet has marveled at the strength, power, flexibility, agility and balance displayed by the gymnasts. Any beginning gymnast who has tried to do a crucifix or planche has been convinced that superhuman strength is required. Any young would-be gymnast running toward the long horse to vault over its length has wished he had more power to insure that he'll clear the far end. Any boy or girl learning the back handspring, walk-over, fore and aft or side splits is convinced that he must develop flexibility if he is to win any medals. All gymnasts are convinced that a good sense of balance, both dynamic and static, are a necessary asset in performing on the balance beam or side horse or when attempting scales, handbalances or levers. Gymnastics is agility personified.

Participation in gymnastics will develop strength, power, flexibility, agility, balance and a measure of endurance. However, a boy or girl who already possesses adequate strength, power and flexibility will learn the gymnastic moves more quickly and with greater safety. He will learn more quickly because lack of adequate strength, power or flexibility will be eliminated as a cause of failure. The causes of failure will be narrowed to incorrect technique, faulty timing or loss of balance. The gymnast will be less likely to suffer injury because he will have the strength necessary to "save" the move. He will be less likely to pull a muscle or suffer a sprain because the range of motion in joints will be greater and the tendons and muscles can be stretched further before being torn.

In gymnastics, strength relative to body weight, not raw strength, is needed. Gymnasts, consequently, have the problem of increasing strength while minimizing weight gains. This is not true in such sports as football, field events and similar sports in which an athlete must move an object or an opponent. The young man or woman with heavily muscled legs and buttocks can never hope to become an outstanding gymnast.

Gymnasts who have difficulty in holding their weight down should diet and do aerobic exercises which have high caloric cost such as jogging, cycling, distance swimming or Cureton's Progressive, Rhythmical, Nonstop Exercises. Gymnastics, however, is an anaerobic activity since routines are of short duration, approximately one minute. In most meets, after each routine there is a rest of approximately five minutes before the gymnast must present his next routine. Endurance work for gymnasts should be of the anaerobic type.

Strength Exercises for Gymnasts

Progressive resistance exercises

60% of maximum athlete can lift in the exercise. 10-15 repetitions for 3-4 sets.

1-1	Military press
1-2	Press behind neck
1-3	Seated military press
1-4	Bench press
1-5	Bent over rowing
1-6	Upright rowing
1-7	Front curl
1-8	Reverse curl
1-9	Lateral exercise
1-10	Triceps exercise
1-11	Supine triceps extension
1-12	Bent arm pull-over
1-13	Wrist curl
1-14	Reverse wrist curl
1-24	Shoulder shrug
1-25	Lateral rise with dumbbells
1-26	Forward rise with dumbbells
1-27	Supine lateral dumbbell raise
1-30	Sit-up

Exercises with the isometric belt

2-1	Military press
2-2	Press behind neck
2-3	Supine press
2-4	Arm depressor
2-5	Front curl
2-6	Reverse curl
2-7	Standing pull-up
2-8	Forward extended arm depressor
2-9	Forward extended arm elevator
2-10	Sideward extended arm depressor
2-11	Sideward extended arm elevator
2-16	Pole vaulter's exercise
2-25	Front shoulder shrug
2-26	Back shoulder shrug
2-27	Chest pull
2-28	Chest push
2-29	Supine extended arm elevator
2-30	Bent over rowing exercise

Isometric exercises with a beach towel

3-1	Military press
3-2	Press behind neck
3-3	Supine press
3-4	Arm depressor
3-5	Front curl
3-6	Reverse curl
3-7	Standing pull-up
3-8	Forward extended arm depressor
3-9	Sideward extended arm depressor
3-10	Forward extended arm elevator
3-11	Sideward extended arm elevator
3-12	Pole vaulter's exercise
3-25	Chest pull
3-30	Supine extended arm elevator
3-31	Pull-over
3-32	Bent over rowing exercise
3-35	Wrist front curl
3-36	Wrist reverse curl

Isometric exercises without equipment

3-37	Extended arm elevator

3-38	Extended arm depressor
3-39	Flexed arm elevator
3-40	Flexed arm depressor
3-41	Forward extended arm sideward mover
3-42	Arm extensor
3-43	Front curl on a desk
3-44	Reverse curl on a desk
3-45	Arm depressor on a desk
3-46	Arm depressor on a chair
3-47	Chair lift
3-48	Parade rest pull
3-49	Overhead pull
3-50	Sideward arm elevator
3-51	Sideward arm depressor
3-52	Forward extended arm elevator
3-53	Pull-over
3-54	Resisted push-up
3-65	Chest push
3-66	Chest pull
3-69	Seated shoulder shrug
3-70	Sit-up with a partner
3-71	Prone back arch with a partner
3-74	Wrist front curl
3-75	Wrist reverse curl
3-76	Wrist pronator and supinator

Endurance Exercises for Gymnasts

It has been pointed out earlier that gymnasts need anaerobic power since their routines last for approximately one minute. They use principally the muscles of the upper body.

A circuit consisting of the following events is recommended. (The reader should review the section on circuit training in Chapter 4.)

1. Push-ups
2. V-sits
3. Back extensions
4. Abdominal curls
5. Sit-ups
6. Pull-ups
7. Trunk twister
8. Dips

9. Press with barbell
10. Curl with barbell
11. Upright rowing

Periodically, the coach should change the events included in the circuit. Some other events which could be included for gymnasts are the following:

1. Press behind neck
2. Bench press
3. Bent over rowing
4. Reverse curls
5. Lateral exercise
6. Triceps exercise
7. Bent arm pull-overs
8. Shoulder shrugs
9. Trunk twisters
10. The bouncer
11. Leg crossovers
12. Flutter kicks on front
13. Flutter kicks on back
14. Chin-ups
15. Leg raisers on stall bars
16. Handstand push-ups against the wall

The coach of gymnastics will find *grass drills* an excellent modality for improving his gymnasts' anaerobic power with a minimal expenditure of time. These should be done at the end of the practice session in order that the resulting fatigue will not interfere with skills learning. Gymnasts should do 6 one-minute bouts with a rest of 2 to 3 minutes between each bout.

Wind sprints can also be adapted to the specialized anaerobic needs of gymnasts. Gymnasts could do 6 to 10 sprints of 100 yards each with a rest of 2 to 3 minutes between each sprint.

Rope skipping is interesting to gymnasts who enjoy the type of challenge provided through learning different rope skipping skills. A demonstration of mass rope skipping will provide an interesting supplement to a gymnastic demonstration. To develop the type of anaerobic power needed in gymnastics, gymnasts should do 6 to 8 one to two minute bouts of fast skipping with 2 to 3 minute rests between bouts.

Agility for Gymnasts

The practice of gymnastic moves is the best procedure for developing the specific type of agility for gymnastics. The movements in gymnastics are so diverse, of such great number and of such great variety that there is little to be gained through devising specific agility drills. Furthermore, in most other sports a ball, racquet or stick must be manipulated with the hands or feet while dodging or moving so that, in effect, agility drills become application of the part-whole method of teaching, enabling the athlete during agility drills to focus his attention on his foot and body movements so that during the game he can give almost undivided attention to the ball or implement.

Balance for Gymnasts

As for agility, the practice of gymnastic moves is the best procedure for developing both static and dynamic balance required in gymnastics. Almost all gymnastic moves require and develop either static or dynamic balance.

Flexibility for Gymnasts

Gymnastics makes great demands upon flexibility. Gymnasts do fore and aft and side splits, backbends, walk-overs, German giant swings, eagle giant swings, tucked and piked somersaults and many other moves which require flexibility for successful completion. Unlike balance and agility, which are probably specific to each specific activity and consequently best developed through practice in the activity, flexibility is best developed through stretching exercises. Inadequate flexibility can prevent a gymnast from learning many moves. The necessary flexibility will be most easily developed through specific stretching exercises. Inadequate hip joint flexibility preventing elevation of the hips above the hands while the feet are still on the floor can prevent accomplishment of a straight arm straight leg press to the handstand. Inadequate hip and back flexibility can cause difficulty in learning the back handspring. Although flexibility will be developed while practicing gymnastic moves, it can be developed faster and without the danger of pulling a muscle or tendon through stretching exercises. Stretching exercises should be done at the start of the practice session.

6-1	Back pull
6-2	Assisted back bend
6-3	Scale push
6-4	Scale bend
6-5	Quadriceps stretcher
6-6	Upper back stretcher
6-7	Spine flexor
6-8	Spine flexor with legs crossed
6-9	The hook
6-10	Praying mantis
6-11	Sitting rotor
6-13	Standing front split
6-14	Torture rack
6-15	Lying assisted leg abductor
6-17	Assisted shoulder hyperflexor
6-18	Assisted shoulder hyperextensor
6-20	Assisted outward rotor
6-21	Assisted inward rotor
6-22	Assisted horizontal extensor-abductor
6-23	Assisted horizontal flexor-adductor
6-25	Assisted plantar-flexor of feet
6-27	Back bend
6-28	Belly out
6-29	Hamstring stretcher
6-30	Hurdler's exercise
6-31	Four point stretch
6-32	Fore and aft split
6-33	Side split
6-37	Sideward V
6-38	Hurdler's stretch
6-44	Plantar flexor
6-45	Sitting leg stretch
6-47	Side bender-side split

CONDITIONING FOR VOLLEYBALL

Volleyball players need power in the arm depressors (spike), wrist flexors (serve and spike), hip and knee extensors and plantar flexors (leaping to spike), arm elevators (underhand pass), arm extensors and shoulder elevators (set-up). They need flexibility in the shoulder joint, hips, wrists and ankles in order to apply thrust against the ball or the floor through a greater range. In today's competitive volleyball, volleyball players need a substantial amount of endurance.

Strength for Volleyball Players

Use 75% of maximum weight which can be lifted. Do 4-6 repetitions in 4-5 sets.

Exercises with barbells

1-1	Military press
1-2	Press behind neck
1-3	Seated military press
1-6	Upright rowing
1-7	Front curl
1-8	Reverse curl
1-11	Supine triceps extension
1-12	Bent arm pull-over
1-14	Front wrist curl
1-18	Squat
1-19	Front squat
1-21	Rise on toes
1-23	Knee extensor
1-24	Shoulder shrug

Exercises with the isometric belt

2-1	Military press
2-2	Press behind neck
2-5	Front curl
2-6	Reverse curl
2-8	Forward extended arm depressor
2-9	Forward extended arm elevator
2-20	Wrist and forearm exercise
2-25	Front shoulder shrug
2-29	Supine extended arm elevator
2-31	Dead lift
2-33	Squat
2-34	Sitting leg extensor
2-42	Rise on toes
2-43	Sitting plantar flexor

Isometric exercises with a towel

3-1	Military press
3-2	Press behind neck
3-5	Front curl
3-6	Reverse curl
3-8	Forward extended arm depressor

3-10	Forward extended arm elevator
3-14	Sitting leg extensor
3-15	Sitting plantar flexor
3-30	Supine extended arm elevator
3-31	Pull-over
3-33	Dead lift
3-35	Wrist front curl

Isometric exercises without equipment

3-38	Extended arm depressor
3-42	Arm extensor
3-43	Front curl on a desk
3-44	Reverse curl on a desk
3-51	Sideward arm depressor
3-54	Resisted push-up
3-55	Sitting knee extensor
3-61	Rise on toes in door frame
3-62	Sitting knee extensor with partner
3-69	Seated shoulder shrug
3-74	Wrist front curl
3-75	Wrist reverse curl

Endurance Exercises for Volleyball Players

A *circuit training* course for volleyball players could include several of the strength exercises done with barbells listed on the pages in this section on conditioning exercises for volleyball players as well as the following exercises:

1. Push-ups
2. Running in place
3. Lateral runs (see p. 110)
4. Dips on the parallel bars
5. Rope skipping
6. Run up and down bleachers
7. Any of the flexibility exercises for volleyball players listed in the following pages of this section.

Players should run the circuit at the end of the practice session. The reader is urged to re-read the section on circuit training on pages 105-115.

Cooper's Aerobics or cycling would also be excellent activities to develop the volleyball player's stammina and endurance.

Agility for Volleyball Players

Textbooks on volleyball describe drills which will develop the specific agilities needed. These will not be described here.

Flexibility for Volleyball Players

6-6	Upper back stretcher
6-7	Spine flexor
6-17	Assisted shoulder hyperflexor
6-22	Assisted horizontal extensor-abductor
6-25	Assisted plantar-flexor of feet
6-29	Hamstring stretcher
6-30	Hurdler's exercise
6-31	Four point stretch
6-34	Inch worm
6-35	Sitting rotor
6-41	Trunk twister
6-42	Standing rotor
6-43	Achilles stretch
6-44	Plantar flexor
6-48	Leg crossover
6-49	Wrist exercises

CONDITIONING FOR SPRINTERS

Sprinters need power in the plantar flexors, knee and hip extensors, extensors of the back and arm elevators. They need anaerobic power. They need flexibility in the ankle, knee, hip and shoulder joints in order that the movements are not made against tight antagonists and so that thrust can be applied against the ground for a greater period of time.

Strength and Power for Sprinters

Use 75% of maximum weight which can be lifted in each exercise. Do 4-6 repetitions in each of 4-5 sets.

Exercises with barbells

1-7	Front curl
1-8	Reverse curl
1-15	Dead lift
1-18	Squat
1-19	Front squat
1-20	Back squat
1-21	Rise on toes

1-23	Knee extensor
1-26	Forward raise with dumbbells
1-29	Good morning exercise
1-30	Sit-up

Exercises with the isometric belt

2-5	Front curl
2-6	Reverse curl
2-9	Forward extended arm elevator
2-13	Bowler's exercise
2-18	Rower's exercise
2-29	Supine extended arm elevator
2-31	Dead lift
2-33	Squat
2-34	Sitting leg extensor
2-40	Side leg extensor
2-42	Rise on toes
2-43	Sitting plantar flexor

Isometric exercises with a towel

3-5	Front curl
3-6	Reverse curl
3-10	Forward extended arm elevator
3-14	Sitting leg extensor
3-15	Sitting plantar flexor
3-21	Side leg extensor
3-30	Supine extended arm elevator
3-33	Dead lift
3-42	Arm extensor
3-43	Front curl on a desk
3-44	Reverse curl on a desk
3-47	Chair lift
3-52	Forward extended arm elevator
3-54	Resisted push-up
3-55	Sitting knee extensor
3-61	Rise on toes in door frame
3-62	Sitting knee extensor with partner
3-68	Seated dead lift
3-71	Prone back arch with partner

Endurance for Sprinters

The sprint is an anaerobic event. In the 100 yard dash a maximal effort is made for 10 to 15 seconds. Oxygen intake cannot begin to match the rate of oxygen consumption. Winning the sprints in either swimming or track depends primarily upon the development of anaerobic power. Consequently, the coaches in these sports have become masters of the techniques for developing this quality and their textbooks cover procedures for conditioning for development of anaerobic power very thoroughly. It would be redundant to cover this topic in this textbook.

Flexibility for Sprinters

6-5	Quadriceps stretcher
6-7	Spine flexor
6-11	Sitting rotor
6-14	Torture rack
6-16	Assisted quadricep stretcher
6-18	Assisted shoulder hyperextensor
6-25	Assisted plantar-flexor of feet
6-28	Belly out
6-29	Hamstring stretcher
6-30	Hurdler's exercise
6-31	Four point stretch
6-34	Inch worm
6-37	Sideward V
6-41	Trunk twister
6-43	Achilles stretch
6-44	Plantar flexor
6-45	The bouncer
6-46	Sitting leg stretch

CONDITIONING FOR THE THROWING EVENTS IN TRACK AND FIELD

Discus, javelin and hammer throwers and shot putters must have powerful ankle, knee, hip, spinal, shoulder, elbow and wrist extensors. They must also have powerful spinal rotors. They need little in endurance. The specific kind of balance and agility needed in these events will be developed through practice in their event. They do need flexibility in the ankle, knee, hip, spine, shoulder and wrist in order to develop thrust through a maximal distance and to avoid having prime movers work against tight antagonists.

Strength and Power for Throwing Events in Track and Field

Use 80% of maximum which can be lifted in each exercise. Do 3-5 repetitions in each of 3-4 sets.

Exercises with barbells

1-1	Military press
1-2	Press behind neck
1-3	Seated military press
1-4	Bench press
1-10	Triceps exercise
1-11	Supine triceps exercise
1-13	Front wrist curl
1-15	Dead lift
1-18	Squat
1-19	Front squat
1-20	Back squat
1-21	Rise on toes
1-23	Knee extensor
1-29	Good morning exercise

Exercises with isometric belt

2-1	Military press
2-2	Press behind neck
2-3	Supine press
2-14	Javelin thrower's exercise
2-15	Shot putter's exercise
2-20	Wrist and forearm exercise
2-28	Chest push
2-31	Dead lift
2-33	Squat
2-34	Sitting leg extensor
2-35	Prone leg extensor
2-40	Side leg extensor
2-42	Rise on toes
2-43	Sitting plantar flexor

Isometric exercises with a towel

3-1	Military press
3-2	Press behind neck
3-3	Supine press
3-14	Sitting leg extensor
3-15	Sitting plantar flexor
3-16	Prone leg extensor
3-21	Side leg extensor
3-33	Dead lift
3-35	Wrist front curl

Isometric exercises without equipment

3-42	Arm extensor
3-54	Resisted push-up
3-55	Sitting knee extensor
3-61	Rise on toes in door frame
3-62	Sitting knee extensor with a partner
3-68	Seated dead lift
3-71	Prone back arch with a partner
3-74	Wrist front curl

Flexibility Exercises for Throwing Events in Track and Field

Field event athletes need good flexibility in the shoulder girdle, as well as in the spinal column in terms of rotation, hyperextension, flexion and lateral flextion in order to provide thrust against the discus, javelin, shot or hammer through the greatest possible distance. The greater their flexibility in these areas, the farther back they can draw the implement and consequently, the greater the distance through which they can generate momentum in the implement. For this reason, the prescribed exercises are those which will develop flexibility in the shoulder girdle and in the spinal column.

6-1	Back Pull
6-2	Assisted Back Bend
6-5	Quadriceps Stretcher
6-6	Upper Back Stretcher
6-7	Spine Flexor
6-9	The Hook
6-11	Sitting Rotor
6-14	Torture Rack
6-17	Assisted Shoulder Hyperflexor
6-18	Assisted Shoulder Hyperextensor
6-22	Assisted Horizontal Extensor Abductor
6-27	Back Bend
6-28	Belly Out
6-29	Hamstring Stretcher
6-30	Hurdlers' Exercise
6-35	Sitting Rotor
6-36	Shoulder and Hip Stretcher
6-39	Hip Abductor Stretch
6-42	Standing Rotor
6-44	Plantar Flexor
6-48	Leg Crossover
6-49	Wrist Exercises

CONDITIONING EXERCISES FOR POLE VAULTERS

The first part of a pole vault is a sprint. The greater the forward speed the pole vaulter can generate during his short sprint, the more force he will have to transfer to upward momentum after he plants his pole and springs upward. The pole vaulter must be able, like a sprinter, high jumper or long jumper, to accelerate quickly. This requires powerful plantor flexors of the feet, knee and hip extensors and extensors of the back as well as flexibility in the ankle and hip joints in order to provide thrust over a greater distance.

The pole vaulter must also have powerful elbow flexors and extensors, shoulder and back muscles and hip flexors. He must acquire this power with minimal weight gain for, like the gymnast, it is not raw strength but strength and power relative to weight that determines his success. The pole vaulter must be able not only to chin himself while flexing his hips to bring his feet upward above his head into a handstand but also to push himself upward by extending his elbows while in the handstand position. Obviously, he applies the kinesiologic principle of accumulation of forces, each successive force being initiated at the point of greatest speed but least acceleration of the proceeding force; nevertheless, he needs great strength relative to his body weight to accomplish this. He also needs good hip flexibility in order to assume a tightly jacknifed position so that his feet will shoot upward close to the pole.

Strength and Power Exercises for the Pole Vaulter

Exercises with barbells

Use 75% of weight which can be lifted. Do 4-6 repetitions in each of 4-5 sets.

1-1	Military press
1-2	Press behind neck
1-3	Seated military press
1-4	Bench press
1-5	Bent over rowing
1-6	Upright rowing
1-7	Front curl
1-8	Reverse curl
1-9	Lat exercise
1-10	Triceps exercise
1-11	Supine triceps exercise

1-12	Bent arm pullover
1-15	Dead lift
1-18	Squat
1-19	Front squat
1-20	Back squat
1-21	Rise on toes
1-23	Knee extensor
1-24	Shoulder shrug
1-29	Good morning exercise
1-30	Sit up

Isometric exercises with isometric belt

2-1	Military press
2-2	Press behind neck
2-3	Supine press
2-4	Arm depressor
2-5	Front curl
2-6	Reverse curl
2-7	Standing pull up
2-8	Forward extended arm depressor
2-16	Pole vaulters' exercise
2-25	Front shoulder shurg
2-26	Back shoulder shrug
2-30	Bent over rowing exercise
2-31	Dead lift
2-33	Squat
2-34	Sitting leg extensor
2-36	Supine hip flexor
2-40	Side leg extensor
2-41	Sitting leg raiser
2-42	Rise on toes
2-43	Sitting plantar flexor

Isometric exercises with a towel

3-1	Military press
3-2	Press behind neck
3-3	Supine press
3-4	Arm depressor
3-5	Front curl
3-6	Reverse curl
3-7	Standing pull up
3-8	Forward extended arm depressor
3-12	Pole vaulters' exercise

3-14	Sitting leg extensor
3-15	Sitting plantar flexor
3-16	Prone leg extensor
3-17	Supine hip flexor
3-21	Side leg extensor
3-31	Pull over
3-32	Bent over rowing exercise
3-33	Dead lift
3-42	Arm extensor
3-43	Front curl on a desk
3-44	Reverse curl on desk
3-45	Arm depressor on a desk
3-53	Pull over
3-55	Sitting knee extensor
3-61	Rise on toes in door frame
3-62	Sitting knee extensor with a partner
3-68	Seated dead lift
3-69	Seated shoulder shrug
3-70	Sit up with a partner

Flexibility Exercises for Pole Vaulters

As he springs from the ground, the pole vaulter must possess full range of motion in the direction of dorsiflexion in order to apply thrust against the ground through a maximal distance. He must possess excellent flexibility in the hip joint, particularly in the direction of flexion of this joint, in order to assume the tightly piked or jacknifed position as he rides the pole upward and brings his feet to head level. After he extends his hips and pushes upward toward the handstand position, he must have good shoulder flexibility in the direction of hyperflexion if he is to bring his trunk into line with his arms.

6-7	Spine Flexor
6-8	Spine Flexor with Legs Crossed
6-9	The Hook
6-10	Praying Mantis
6-17	Assisted Shoulder Hyperflexor
6-24	Assisted Plantar Flexor of Feet
6-29	Hamstring Stretcher
6-30	Hurdlers' Exercise
6-31	Four Point Stretch
6-34	Inch Worm
6-36	Shoulder and Hip Stretcher
6-37	Sideward V

6-43	Achilles Stretch
6-44	Plantar Flexor
6-45	The Bouncer
6-46	Sitting Leg Stretcher

CONDITIONING EXERCISES FOR LACROSSE PLAYERS

Lacrosse players need good anaerobic power since this is a game of numerous sprints over a field of 110 yards by 60-70 yards. They must also possess a measure of aerobic power, since the game is sixty minutes in length with four fifteen minute quarters with a ten minute interval at half time and only one minute between the first and second and the third and fourth quarters.

Lacrosse players need good power in the arm and shoulder extensors and flexors since when throwing the ball with the stick they extend the upper arm and flex the lower arm. They also need powerful legs since they are called upon to do many sprints. To provide thrust over a greater distance, they should possess good flexibility in the shoulders and wrists. They should also possess good flexibility in the spinal rotors in order to twist away from opponents.

Strength and Power Exercises for Lacrosse Players

Exercises with Barbells: Use 50% of maximum weight which can be lifted in each exercise. Do 15-20 repetitions in each of 2-3 sets.

1-1	Military Press
1-2	Press Behind Neck
1-4	Bench Press
1-7	Front Curl
1-8	Reverse Curl
1-10	Triceps Exercise
1-11	Supine Triceps Extension
1-13	Front Wrist Curl
1-14	Reverse Wrist Curl
1-18	Squat
1-19	Front Squat
1-20	Back Squat
1-21	Rise on Toes
1-23	Knee Extensor

Exercises with the isometric belt

2-1	Military Press
2-2	Press Behind Neck

2-3	Supine Press
2-5	Front Curl
2-6	Reverse Curl
2-8	Forward Extended Arm Depressor
2-9	Forward Extended Arm Elevator
2-18	Rowers' Exercise
2-20	Wrist and Forearm Exercise
2-27	Chest Pull
2-28	Sideward Push
2-29	Supine Extended Arm Elevator
2-31	Dead Lift
2-32	Chest Push
2-33	Squat
2-34	Sitting Leg Extensor
2-35	Prone Leg Extensor
2-37	Sitting Leg Abductor
2-38	Sitting Leg Adductor
2-40	Side Leg Extensor
2-41	Sitting Leg Raiser
2-42	Rise on Toes
2-43	Sitting Plantar Flexor
2-45	Sitting Foot Adductor
2-46	Sitting Foot Abductor

Isometric exercises with a towel

3-1	Military Press
3-2	Press Behind Neck
3-3	Supine Press
3-5	Front Curl
3-6	Reverse Curl
3-8	Forward Extended Arm Depressor
3-10	Forward Extended Arm Elevator
3-14	Sitting Leg Extensor
3-16	Prone Leg Extensor
3-18	Sitting Leg Abductor
3-19	Sitting Foot Abductor
3-21	Side Leg Extensor
3-22	Sitting Leg Adductor
3-23	Sitting Foot Adductor
3-30	Supine Extended Arm Elevator
3-33	Dead Lift
3-34	Suitcase Lift
3-35	Wrist Front Curl
3-36	Wrist Reverse Curl

Isometric exercises without equipment

3-42	Arm Extensor
3-43	Front Curl on a Desk
3-44	Reverse Curl on a Desk
3-45	Arm Depressor on a Desk
3-52	Forward Extended Arm Elevator
3-54	Resisted Push Up
3-55	Sitting Knee Extensor
3-56	Sitting Leg Adductor
3-57	Sitting Leg Abductor
3-59	Foot Abductor
3-60	Foot Adductor
3-61	Rise on Toes in Door Frame
3-62	Sitting Knee Extensor with Partner
3-64	Ankle Eversion and Inversion with Partner
3-68	Seated Dead Lift
3-70	Sit Up with a Partner
3-73	Lying Side Leg Raiser
3-74	Wrist Front Curl
3-75	Wrist Reverse Curl
3-76	Wrist Pronator and Supinator

Endurance Exercises for Lacrosse Players

The nature of lacrosse drills and play is such that players can improve their endurance during practice while simultaneously improving their stick handling ability. Play is strenuous, calling for much jogging and repeated sprints while the coordinations are not so fine that skill will be greatly impaired when fatigue sets in, nor are hazards so great as to militate against drill and scrimmage so conducted as to utilize the overload principle. Drills with 5 on 3, 3 on 2, or 2 on 1 can be continued to the point of substantial fatigue increasing their duration at each practice session. Textbooks on lacrosse contain descriptions of many drills which can be utilized to simultaneously improve skills and endurance. These can be supplemented at the end of the practice session with rope skipping, grass drills, wind sprints, or jogging around the field.

Flexibility Exercises for Lacrosse Players

Lacrosse players need flexibility in the ankle joints in order to provide thrust against the ground for a greater distance when running and to decrease the probability of suffering an ankle sprain. They need flexibility in the tendons of the muscles of the thigh and hip in order to decrease the probability of suffering a groin strain or pulled thigh muscle and in order to cut, pivot and turn with greater facility and less resistance from tight antagonists. They need flexibility in the spinal rotors for the same reason. They need flexibility in the shoulder area and wrists in order to manipulate the stick through a greater range of motion to impart thrust for a greater distance and in order to move their stick out of the reach of an opponent in close play.

6-5	Quadriceps Stretcher
6-6	Upper Back Stretcher
6-11	Sitting Rotor
6-15	Lying Assisted Leg Abductor
6-16	Assisted Quadricep Stretcher
6-17	Assisted Shoulder Hyperflexor
6-18	Assisted Shoulder Hyperextensor
6-19	Assisted Shoulder Abductor
6-22	Assisted Horizontal Extensor-Abductor
6-25	Assisted Plantar Flexor of Feet
6-26	Assisted Supinator and Pronator of Feet
6-28	Belly Out
6-29	Hamstring Stretcher
6-30	Hurdlers' Exercise
6-31	Four Point Stretch
6-34	Inch Worm
6-35	Sitting Rotor
6-36	Shoulder and Hip Stretcher
6-41	Trunk Twister
6-42	Standing Rotor
6-43	Achilles' Stretch
6-44	Plantar Flexor
6-45	The Bouncer
6-48	Leg Crossover
6-49	Wrist Exercises

CONDITIONING EXERCISES FOR SOCCER PLAYERS

Soccer players need powerful hip flexors, knee extensors and dorsiflexors in order to kick the ball with force. Halfbacks and forwards also need strong adductors and abductors in order to change directions, and cut and dodge quickly. All soccer players need strong neck muscles in order to head to the ball with force. They need good flexibility in ankles and hips to apply thrust through a greater distance when kicking and good flexibility in the spinal rotors in order to spin away from would-be tacklers. They need good anaerobic endurance.

Strength Exercises for Soccer Players

Exercises with barbells

1-15	Dead Lift
1-18	Squat
1-19	Front Squat
1-20	Back Squat
1-21	Rise on Toes
1-22	Leg Curl
1-23	Knee Extensor
1-24	Shoulder Shurg
1-29	Good Morning Exercise
1-30	Sit Up
1-31	Neck Flexor

Exercises with the isometric belt

2-18	Rowers' Exercise
2-21	Forward Push (Neck)
2-22	Backward Push (Neck)
2-23	Sideward Push (Neck)
2-24	Head Turn (Neck)
2-25	Front Shoulder Shrug
2-26	Back Shoulder Shrug
2-30	Bent Over Rowing Exercise
2-31	Dead Lift
2-33	Squat
2-34	Sitting Leg Extensor
2-35	Prone Leg Extensor
2-36	Supine Hip Flexor
2-37	Sitting Leg Abductor
2-38	Sitting Leg Adductor
2-39	Side Leg Flexor
2-40	Side Leg Extensor
2-41	Sitting Leg Raiser
2-42	Rise on Toes
2-43	Sitting Plantar Flexor
2-44	Sitting Dorsal Flexor
2-45	Sitting Foot Adductor
2-46	Sitting Foot Abductor

Isometric exercises with a towel

3-14	Sitting Leg Extensor
3-15	Sitting Plantar Flexor
3-16	Prone Leg Extensor
3-17	Supine Hip Flexor
3-18	Sitting Leg Abductor
3-19	Sitting Foot Abductor
3-20	Side Leg Flexor
3-21	Side Leg Extensor
3-22	Sitting Leg Adductor
3-23	Sitting Foot Adductor
3-24	Sitting Dorsal Flexor
3-26	Head Forward Push
3-27	Head Backward Push
3-28	Head Sideward Push
3-29	Head Turn
3-33	Dead Lift

Isometric exercises without equipment

3-55	Sitting Knee Extensor
3-56	Sitting Leg Adductor
3-57	Sitting Leg Abductor
3-58	Dorsi Flexor on Desk
3-59	Foot Abductor
3-60	Foot Adductor
3-61	Rise on Toes in Door Frame
3-62	Sitting Knee Extensor with Partner
3-63	Sitting Knee Flexor with Partner
3-64	Ankle Eversion and Inversion with Partner
3-67	Neck Exercises
3-70	Sit-Up With Partner
3-73	Lying Resisted Side Leg Raiser

Endurance Exercises for Soccer Players

A number of drills have been developed in soccer which develop the specific kind of agility, dynamic balance and anaerobic endurance needed in this game. The soccer coach will be acquainted with a number of these drills such as one-on-one, two-on-three or three-on-three. Through these drills players can develop endurance while improving their dribbling, passing, trapping, and tackling skills. Top level endurance will do the player little good unless he can control the ball. However, a tired player doesn't coordinate very well. It is necessary that the coach make a judgment on each player to determine whether the player needs more to develop skill or to develop endurance. If he makes more errors in the last part of the game, it is likely that fatigue is having a detrimental effect upon his performance. If this is the case, the player needs endurance work more than he does work on skills.

In soccer there are four quarters of twenty-two minutes each and the field is 120 yds. by 75 yds. This is a large area! Furthermore, play is almost continuous. However, individual players intersperse bursts of activity with a slower pace. The player usually sprints about fifteen yards for a tackle, dribbles about fifteen yards and then passes to another player. He may then sprint again to place himself in position to receive a pass. An endurance exercise for soccer players could involve fifteen and twenty yard sprints at various angles alternating with fifteen twenty yard jogs or walks repeated until a total distance of a mile or more has been covered.

Flexibility Exercises for Soccer Players

Soccer players need good flexibility in the ankles and hips in order to apply thrust against the ball through a greater distance. They also need good flexibility in the spinal rotors in order to avoid tacklers and to turn to meet oncoming balls or to send the ball in a new direction.

6-3	Scale Push
6-4	Scale Bend
6-5	Quadriceps Stretcher
6-7	Spine Flexor
6-8	Spine Flexor with Legs Crossed
6-10	Praying Mantis
6-11	Sitting Rotor
6-13	Standing Front Split
6-15	Lying Assisted Leg Abductor
6-24	Assisted Dorsi Flexor of Feet
6-25	Assisted Plantar Flexor of Feet
6-26	Assisted Supinator and Pronator of Feet
6-29	Hamstring Stretcher
6-30	Hurdlers' Exercise
6-31	Four Point Stretch
6-34	Inch Worm

6-35	Sitting Rotor
6-37	Sideward V
6-39	Hip Abductor Stretch
6-40	Hip Adductor Stretch
6-41	Trunk Twister
6-42	Standing Rotor
6-43	Achilles Stretch
6-44	Plantar Flexor
6-45	The Bouncer
6-46	Sitting Leg Stretch
6-48	Leg Crossover

WRESTLING

In all weight classes with the exception of the unlimited class and perhaps to a lesser degree in the 191 pound class, wrestling demands great strength relative to body weight. No other sport except gymnastics places as high a premium on strength relative to body weight as does wrestling. Every muscle is used and every muscle must be powerfully developed. A wrestler can sometimes escape from a pinning combination if his strength is adequate to overcome the advantages of leverage and position of his opponent.

Sometimes a surprising degree of flexibility will also enable a wrestler to escape a pinning combination. Whether he is on offense or defense, a wrestler needs great agility and a fine sense of dynamic balance. The wrestler with good flexibility can often "give" enough to his opponent's force to prevent a pin. Furthermore, a substantial degree of flexibility will decrease the probability of the wrestler suffering a sprain or pulled muscle. The advisability of the wrestler possessing great agility and a fine sense of dynamic balance seems so obvious as to appear ridiculous to attempt to justify. Not only is the wrestler who is off balance unlikely to effect a pin but he will, in all probability, be pinned.

In collegiate competition, matches last a total of eight minutes —two periods of three minutes and one period of two minutes. Everything else being equal, the wrestler who is least fatigued at the end of each period and at the end of the match, will win because his reflexes will be quicker, his actions will be more accurate and he will be able to exert the most force.

Strength Exercises for Wrestlers

Exercises with barbells and dumbbells

Use 60% of maximum weight which can be lifted in the particular exercise. Do 10-15 repetitions in each of 3-4 sets.

1-1	Military Press
1-2	Press Behind Neck
1-3	Seated Military Press
1-4	Bench Press
1-5	Bent Over Rowing
1-6	Upright Rowing
1-7	Front Curl
1-8	Reverse Curl
1-11	Supine Triceps Extension
1-12	Bent Arm Pull Over
1-15	Dead Lift
1-18	Squat
1-21	Rise on Toes
1-22	Leg Curl
1-24	Shoulder Shrug
1-25	Lateral Rise with Dumbbells
1-26	Forward Rise with Dumbbells
1-29	Good Monring Exercise
1-30	Sit Up
1-31	Neck Flexor

Exercises with the isometric belt

2-1	Military Press
2-2	Press Behind Neck
2-3	Supine Press
2-4	Arm Depressor
2-5	Front Curl
2-6	Reverse Curl
2-7	Standing Pull Up
2-18	Rowers' Exercise
2-19	Pull Over
2-20	Wrist and Forearm Exercise
2-21	Forward Push (Neck)
2-22	Backward Push (Neck)
2-23	Sideward Push (Neck)
2-24	Head Turn (Neck)
2-25	Front Shoulder Shrug

2-27	Chest Pull
2-28	Sideward Push (Chest)
2-29	Supine Extended Arm Elevator
2-30	Bent Over Rowing Exercise
2-31	Dead Lift
2-32	Suitcase Lift
2-33	Squat
2-34	Sitting Leg Extensor
2-37	Sitting Leg Abductor
2-38	Sitting Leg Adductor
2-42	Rise on Toes

Isometric exercises with a beach towel, partner or without equipment

3-1	Military Press
3-2	Press Behind Neck
3-3	Supine Press
3-4	Arm Depressor
3-5	Front Curl
3-6	Reverse Curl
3-7	Standing Pull Up
3-12	Pole Vaulters' Exercise
3-14	Sitting Leg Extensor
3-15	Sitting Plantar Flexor
3-18	Sitting Leg Abductor
3-22	Sitting Leg Adductor
3-25	Chest Pull
3-26	Head Forward Push
3-27	Head Backward Push
3-28	Head Sideward Push
3-29	Head Turn
3-30	Supine Extended Arm Elevator
3-31	Pull Over
3-32	Bent Over Rowing Exercise
3-33	Dead Lift
3-34	Suitcase Lift
3-42	Arm Extensor
3-43	Front Curl on a Desk
3-44	Reverse Curl on a Desk
3-47	Chair Lift
3-48	Parade Rest Pull
3-49	Overhead Pull

3-53	Pull Over
3-56	Sitting Leg Adductor
3-57	Sitting Leg Abductor
3-61	Rise on Toes in Door Frame
3-65	Chest Push
3-66	Chest Pull
3-67	Neck Exercises
3-68	Seated Dead Lift
3-69	Seated Shoulder Shrug
3-70	Sit Up with a Partner
3-71	Prone Back Arch with a Partner
3-73	Lying Resisted Side Leg Raiser
3-74	Wrist Front Curl
3-75	Wrist Reverse Curl
3-76	Wrist Pronator and Supinator

Endurance Exercises for Wrestlers

Competitive wrestling requires great muscular and cardio-respiratory endurance. Eight minutes of intensive one-on-one in wrestling is probably one of the most stressful of activities. There is no time when the ball is on the other end of the field as in baseball, football, basketball or soccer. The wrestler can rest when he is riding or being ridden but if he spends much time doing this, he won't win many wrestling matches. He must be able to at least, engage in frequent bursts of extremely strenuous activity and to continue this pace for eight minutes. His goal should be to be able to wrestle intensively for the full eight minutes.

Circuit Training

A circuit for wrestlers could include the following:

1. Parallel Bar Dips—All Out
2. Bridge Spin-outs—10
3. Push Ups—All Out
4. V-Sits—All Out
5. Back Extensions—10-50
6. Chin-ups—All Out
7. Abdominal Curls—20-60
8. Extension Push-ups—All Out
9. Front Curl with Barbell—3 repetitions 75% of maximum

10. Military Press with Barbell—3 repetitions 75% of maximum
11. Half Squat—5 repetitions 75% of maximum (have 2 spotters)
12. Supine Press with Barbell—3 repetitions 75% of maximum (have 2 spotters)
13. Rope Skipping until 3 minutes of time elapsed since beginning the circuit.

Grass Drills

Three three-minute bouts of grass drills could be incorporated into the conditioning work by having the wrestler do sit-outs, spins, simulated take-downs, etc., on command instead of "front," "back," "right," "left" as described in Chapter 4. One of the team members can lead this drill as he executes the maneuvers in the center of the circle with the team.

Rope Skipping

Rope skipping could be utilized to develop both anaerobic and aerobic power by doing three three-minute bouts of rope skipping. Time should be progressively increased from one to one and a half to two to two and a half to three minutes for each bout as the team members' physical condition improves. Two bouts could be increased to three. Finally, a competitive element could be introduced by having each team member count the turns of his rope to see who has the greatest total at the end of three bouts.

Jogging

Wrestlers should do some jogging to develop aerobic power. This should be done on the wrestlers own time rather than during the formal practice period due to the time consuming nature of this activity.

Balance Exercises for Wrestlers

5-26	Cat Walk Forward on the Balance Beam
5-27	Cat Walk Backward on the Balance Beam
5-32	Cat Walk Sideward on the Balance Beam
5-33	Walk Across the Beam Carrying Another Athlete "Piggy Back"
5-34	Wheelbarrow Walk Across the Beam
5-35	Head Wrestling on the Balance Beam
5-36	Rooster Fight
5-37	Indian Hand Wrestle